NOV 1 2 2015

the pop classic series

it doesn't suck.
suck.
showgirls
adam
nayman

ecwpress

Editors for the press:
Crissy Calhoun and Jennifer Knoch
Cover and text design: David Gee

Library and Archives Canada
Cataloguing in Publication

Nayman, Adam, author
It doesn't suck : Showgirls / Adam Nayman.

(Pop classics ; 1)
Issued in print and electronic formats.
ISBN 978-1-77041-174-6 (pbk.)
Also issued as: 978-1-77090-512-2 (pdf);
978-1-77090-513-9 (epub)

1. Showgirls (Motion picture). 2. Verhoeven,
Paul, 1938– –Criticism and interpretation.
I. Title.

PN1997.S4783N39 2014
791.43'72   C2013-907771-5
C2013-907772-3

The lyrics on page 10 are from the song
"Singer-Songwriter" by Okkervil River and
are reproduced with permission.

Printing: Webcom 5 4 3 2 1
PRINTED AND BOUND IN CANADA

The publication of It Doesn't Suck has been generously supported by the Canada Council for
the Arts which last year invested $157 million to bring the arts to Canadians throughout the
country, and by the Ontario Arts Council (OAC), an agency of the Government of Ontario,
which last year funded 1,681 individual artists and 1,125 organizations in 216 communities
across Ontario for a total of $52.8 million. We also acknowledge the financial support of the
Government of Canada through the Canada Book Fund for our publishing activities, and the
contribution of the Government of Ontario through the Ontario Book Publishing Tax Credit and
the Ontario Media Development Corporation.

Contents

1

"Masterpiece."

In August 2012, I went out for drinks in Toronto with Mia Hansen-Løve, a talented young French director whom I'd recently profiled for the *Globe and Mail*. I liked her movies, but I was most eager to meet her as a fellow film critic. Before becoming a director, Mia had written reviews for the legendary French publication *Cahiers du Cinéma*. This change in vocation placed her in a long national tradition of film critics turned filmmakers that stretched back to Jean-Luc Godard, François Truffaut, and Eric Rohmer in the 1950s, and more recently included her husband, the gifted writer-director Olivier Assayas.

I also knew that Mia was a fan of the films of Stanley Kubrick and had just cited *Eyes Wide Shut* (1999) on her ballot for the British film journal *Sight & Sound*'s decennial poll of the greatest movies ever made. Because I had recently finished teaching an adult-education course on Kubrick's oeuvre, *Eyes Wide Shut* was on my mind even more than usual, and I thought that it'd be fun to talk about it with somebody who liked it as much as I did. (Actually, she liked it more than I did: the Kubrick movie I'd picked for my own *Sight & Sound* ballot was *2001: A Space Odyssey* [1968], a more conservative choice.)

We did end up talking about movies and comparing notes on our favorites. Eventually, the conversation settled on a film that we both admired very much: an epically scaled Hollywood production from the 1990s with fluid camerawork and a surreally rendered all-American location; an epic erotic comedy populated by an ensemble of leering, lecherous men and nubile naked women; a famous flop that generated plenty of idle gossip and dismissive giggles en route to being rediscovered as a modern classic. But that movie was not *Eyes Wide Shut*. Instead, I discovered that Mia was a great and devoted fan of Paul Verhoeven's *Showgirls* (1995).

Imagine my delight at meeting a fellow traveler! Mia also told me that she'd included a scene about *Showgirls* in the screenplay for her next movie, *Eden*:

Arnaud's apartment. Int. Night

Scenes on a TV screen from the Paul Verhoeven movie Showgirls. Slumped on a couch or in an armchair: J-C, Guillaume and Anne-Claire, Cyril, Paul, Arnaud, and MIDORI, his new girlfriend. End credits. Arnaud gets up, finds the remote, and shuts off the DVD player.

ARNAUD

Showgirls. Masterpiece.

ANNE-CLAIRE

Junk!

CYRIL

I'd even say: trash.

ANNE-CLAIRE

*Seriously the actress could be nominated for the worst
actress of all time.*

GUILLAUME

She got several Razzies.

MIDORI

What are Razzies?

GUILLAUME

Prizes for worst actress of the year. Oscars, but negative.

ARNAUD

*I guess you're referring to her at times over-the-top
performance.*

GUILLAUME

That's putting it mildly.

ARNAUD

But it's on purpose! Verhoeven directs her like that to
emphasize his take on things. He accentuates the mon-
strosity. He's targeting the vulgarity of the United States.
This is the third time I've shown it to you and you still
don't understand. It's pathetic!

J-C

Which is why I suggest we move on.

ANNE-CLAIRE

You take advantage of us each time. We're totally
exhausted. You could show us any crap you want.

ARNAUD

But it's not crap. It's the masterpiece of the '90s.

PAUL

I'd take the middle road: it's not the piece of junk critics
said it was when it came out. It's still Verhoeven, but not
one of his better ones.

CYRIL

Pfff. The movie is a piece of shit. You're crazy.
(He stands up and goes for his cigarettes.)

In his essay "Beaver Las Vegas," critic I.Q. Hunter writes
that "Paul Verhoeven's lap-dance musical *Showgirls* is that rare

object in cultural life: a film universally derided as 'bad.' No one seems to like it. At a time of alleged cultural relativism and collapsing standards of aesthetic judgment, *Showgirls* has emerged as a welcome gold standard of poor taste and world-class incompetence."[1] Hunter was writing in 2000, when most of the people who talked about *Showgirls* probably sounded like Cyril. Nearly 15 years later, there are more and more people who would side with Arnaud.

This swing makes *Showgirls* an even rarer bird than Hunter suggests. It is a film that, previously universally derided as "bad," is now widely suspected of being "good." (It even received a single, lonely vote on that aforementioned *Sight & Sound* poll, from Greek director David Panos, who slotted it alongside Andrei Tarkovsky's *Mirror* [1975] and Orson Welles's *Touch of Evil* [1958].)[2] Film canons are built and guarded as sturdily as fortresses, but intruders sometimes slip through the back door. Once a ratified anti-classic to rank with the likes of *Plan 9 from Outer Space* (1959) or *Valley of the Dolls* (1967) on lists of the worst movies ever made, *Showgirls* has now become the beneficiary of shifting critical polarities, revered both at the "low" end of pop culture as a hardy cult favorite, and at the "high" end by academics as a critical fetish object. Its diverse defenders include feminist theorists, drag queens, old-school auteurists, and octogenarian superstars of the French New Wave, and there's nary an apologist among them — because, as Ryan O'Neal and Ali MacGraw reminded us in *Love Story*, love means never having to say you're sorry.

The attitudes toward *Showgirls* may have changed, but the

movie has not. It has not been re-edited into a "Director's Cut" like *Blade Runner* (1982) or *Apocalypse Now* (1979), to cite two examples of major (and majorly flawed) movies that have over the years required "rescuing" from their imperfect original incarnations. It has not been re-released on DVD with a bevy of additional scenes lifted from the cutting-room floor, which might have implicated studio tampering or an overzealous editor as the cause of the film's derided original version. It has been edited for television and home video, but only to trim the naughty bits: the film's stately parade of both scantily and entirely unclad young women had finally earned Verhoeven the verboten NC-17 rating he'd managed to avoid for his previous boundary-pushing hits *RoboCop* (1987) and *Basic Instinct* (1992).

Showgirls has the same running time now that it did when it premiered on September 22, 1995: it is 131 minutes long (including credits), which makes it shorter than an average Best Picture winner from the 1990s and longer than any of its fellow Razzie Award winners for Worst Picture except for *The Postman* (1997) and *Transformers: Revenge of the Fallen* (2009). It is still organized as a guided tour of pre-millennial Las Vegas in the company of burger-scarfing exotic dancers, tyrannical choreographers, callow rock stars, and coke-snorting hotel executives. It still features a trick brassiere, several runaway chimpanzees, and a scene about the professional ethics of applying ice cubes to a dancer's nipples. And it still begins and ends with a young woman hitching a ride by the side of a crowded superhighway.

2

Through the Looking Glass

When we first see Nomi Malone (Elizabeth Berkley) in *Showgirls*, she's thumbing a lift to Las Vegas. In the last scene of the movie, she's getting the hell out of town. The two scenes are mirror images of one another, and *Showgirls* as a whole is filled with mirrors. There are the deluxe models that dominate the lavish suites at the chic Stardust Hotel, providing a panoply of reflected perspectives on Nomi and her idol/mentor/ rival Cristal Connors (Gina Gershon) as they stalk each other through their backstage power play cum seduction. There are the more functional row mirrors, adorned with tacked-up personal items and Polaroids of loved ones, that the secondary performers in the Stardust's various soft-core musical spectaculars use to apply make-up before and in between production numbers. There are the smaller, dirtier, dingier versions of the same at the more down-market flesh fair the Cheetah Club, these mirrors topped by a proprietary neon sign reading "Al's Girls" so that his employees can quite literally reflect on their job status as they prepare to shake their moneymakers at businessmen and tourists.

The importance of mirrors in *Showgirls* extends beyond the set decoration, however. Ideas of reflection and doubling are present at every level of the filmmaking. The first time that Nomi sees Cristal perform, she mirrors her gestures exactly from her spot on the balcony, as if indicating her desire to take the older woman's place. In another scene, Nomi and Cristal begin unconsciously imitating each other's hand movements as they talk over lunch at Spago. There are numerous scenes in which choreographers instruct dancers to follow their lead: the mantra of the Stardust's house choreographer Marty (Patrick Bristow) is "in sync!" which he bellows as he surveys the mechanized movements of his charges. Most of the female characters have two names: their given names and their more colorful stage monikers.

Even the film's two most infamously sleazy sequences are a matching set. In the first, Nomi delivers an extremely athletic lap dance at the Cheetah Club to Cristal's boyfriend (and the Stardust's entertainment director) Zack Carey (Kyle MacLachlan), who helplessly ejaculates in his pants and limps off into the night. Later on, Nomi repeats the dry-hump choreography almost exactly while actually having sex with Zack in his private outdoor swimming pool, underneath a fountain sculpted in the shape of a breaching dolphin.

Showgirls is rife with such two-for-one effects — it even pauses on two separate occasions to watch Nomi tuck into some fast-food French fries — and yet for many viewers, the film boils down to the clear binary opposition embodied by Cyril and Arnaud in Hansen-Løve's screenplay. Either *Showgirls* is a piece of shit — the received wisdom, and for a long time the majority view — or it's some sort of trashy masterpiece, which is the revisionist claim. Behind Door # 3, however, lies the tantalizing possibility that the movie might be both at the same time, a masterpiece that is somehow also a Piece of Shit. This third option is especially attractive to those who believe or condone the idea that something can be so bad that it's good — that it is possible to derive pleasure from an inept work of art not in spite of its shortcomings, but because of them.

This is the territory marked out by Susan Sontag in her landmark 1964 essay "Notes on 'Camp,'" which sought to codify an amorphous and free-floating aesthetic sensibility and instead set off a half-century's worth of debate. "The ultimate camp statement," according to Sontag, is "it's good *because* it's awful."[3] Coming at the end of a manifesto that already flies off in several different directions, this contradiction is a conceptual crevasse: a taxonomical space broad and deep and inviting enough to accommodate countless scores of movies, books, songs, and other misfit cultural objects seeking a cozy theoretical niche to call their own.

In their 2008 song "Singer-Songwriter," the Austin-based indie-rock band Okkervil River tunefully encapsulate this position in lead singer Will Sheff's contradictory account of a movie he'd seen with some friends. "This film we once saw was reviled for its flaws / But its flaws were what made us have fun," he sings against the sound of Charles Bissell's driving guitar, affirming the notion of time well wasted. The flawed, reviled movie in question is never named; for all we know, it might have been *Showgirls*, and Sheff's narrator might have seen it at exactly the sort of late-night séance arranged by Arnaud. Or perhaps it was at the behest of a less sympathetic host like Martin Codd, the New York City club promoter who told the *New York Times* in March 1996, "There can be nothing more hilarious than getting drunk and watching *Showgirls*."[4] Codd tested out his assumption by holding screenings at his Hell's Kitchen apartment. The image that emerges from the *Times* story is that of a sadistic ceremony, a midnight movie mass where a guilty film is dragged out of the shadows and chained up center stage for all to see.

Is it really possible, though, to kill something that's already dead? *Showgirls* expired meekly at the box office. Its domestic theatrical gross of $35 million in its initial release was extremely disappointing in relation to its $40 million budget and to Verhoeven's previous American productions *RoboCop*, *Total Recall* (1990), and *Basic Instinct*, which had each been among the top earners of their respective years. *Showgirls* was also D.O.A. with critics, who saw a vulnerable target and did quick-hit executions of virtually everybody associated with the film. The most lethal bullets were reserved for Verhoeven, screenwriter Joe Eszterhas, and star Elizabeth Berkley, who absorbed the fire like Sonny Corleone stopped at the toll-booth in *The Godfather* (1972) — although perhaps a more apt comparison would be Sofia Coppola in *The Godfather: Part III* (1990), who took the bullets meant for her father(s) onscreen and off. "She can't act, but watching her try to act, to do the things acting is rumored to consist of, is moving," wrote Anthony Lane in his typically glib evisceration of *Showgirls* in the *New Yorker*.[5] Compared to some other writers, he was being kind.

The definitive public eulogy was delivered by the Golden Raspberry Awards Foundation, which bestowed a record seven Razzies on the film, including Worst Picture, Worst Director, and Worst Actress. Showing unprecedented chutzpah, Verhoeven bucked tradition by accepting his statu-ette in person. "When I was making movies in Holland, my films were judged by the critics as decadent, perverted, and sleazy," he joked. "So I moved to the United States. This was ten years ago. In the meantime, my movies are criticized as being decadent, perverted, and sleazy in *this* country."[6] If the grieving period for the director was brief, it was non-existent for everyone else. Over the next few years, in a series of tell-all articles and books — most prominently Eszterhas's 2006 showbiz memoir *The Devil's Guide to Hollywood* — even mem-bers of the immediate family took their turn to speak ill of the deceased.

The continued abuse of a movie that had already been rel-egated to the slab could be taken as profaning a corpse. But it was on the midnight-movie circuit — a place where the occult

is taken seriously and vampires and zombies feel at home —
that *Showgirls* began its rise from the grave. Though few people
wanted to see *Showgirls* when it was in theaters, on home video
it became a curiosity, and then a minor group-viewing phe-
nomenon. Starting in 1996, MGM graciously offered prints to
repertory theaters, and then hired drag queens to attend the
screenings and encourage audience participation.

Suddenly, *Showgirls*' major reference point had shifted
from *Valley of the Dolls* to *The Rocky Horror Picture Show* (1975).
"A performer named Winona, in a black vinyl miniskirt and
bustier, passed out scripts that cued viewers . . . when to shout
along with the dopiest lines," reported the *New York Times*.
"The movie rolled, accompanied by non-stop shouted wise-
cracks. When Nomi threw a pile of French fries during a dramatic scene, a heckler yelled 'Overact, Nomi!'"[7] MGM had
allowed their intellectual property to be reduced to a punch
line, but in the end, the studio laughed all the way to the bank.
The various re-releases shored up *Showgirls*' box-office take
until it became, with all revenue streams accounted for, one
of the most profitable titles in the studio's back catalogue. To
date, *Showgirls* has grossed more than $100 million. To quote
the film's loquacious screenwriter: "Remember that chicken
shit can turn into chicken liver."[8]

That line is classic Joe Eszterhas, but transubstantiation
is generally considered to be a more sacred process. For one
thing, you need some high priests. In spring 2003, as MGM
was repackaging *Showgirls* as an ironic and fully interactive
home-entertainment experience, the American journal *Film*

Quarterly found space for a 16-page "roundtable" on the film. "It sounds like the setup for a punch line about those wacky academics who find value in any kind of popular culture," snarked *Salon's* film critic Charles Taylor, calling the confab "the perfect new joke for people who realize that their old gibes about the French and Jerry Lewis are getting a little tatty at the edges."[9]

Leaving aside the fact that Taylor's own gibes about academics are themselves rather tatty at the edges, his invocation of a Gallic tradition is correct, especially in regard to prevailing trends in film criticism. The long lineage of French critics turned directors had often been marked by the various cohorts' enthusiastic endorsement of American popular moviemaking. François Truffaut's 1954 essay "A Certain Tendency of the French Cinema" yielded the concept of a *politique des auteurs*, which was adapted and codified by the American critic Andrew Sarris, in his landmark book *The American Cinema*, as the "auteur theory." At its root, the auteur theory holds that the director, more than any other member of a production, is the "author" and guiding intelligence of every film on which she works, scrawling each with a recognizable signature.

Both the *politique* and theory of auteurism resulted in a sea change in critical values. Where mainstream American and British critics of the 1950s were content to praise Alfred Hitchcock as a competent entertainer, French auteurists like future filmmakers Éric Rohmer and Claude Chabrol saw him as working through a constellation of recurring themes and visual ideas. Jean-Luc Godard waxed rhapsodic about the taut genre pictures of Howard Hawks and the florid Technicolor melodramas of Nicholas Ray, whom he memorably designated as the living embodiment of what moviemaking might aspire to. ("The cinema is Nicholas Ray," he wrote.) And in this same spirit, it was the French director Jacques Rivette — a colleague and contemporary of both Truffaut and Godard, whose half-century-and-counting career has been dotted by eccentric masterpieces like *Celine and Julie Go Boating* (1974) and the mammoth 13-hour Balzac riff *Out 1* (1971) — who really got the ball rolling on the critical rehabilitation of *Showgirls*.

In 1998, Rivette sat for an interview with Frédéric Bonnaud for the French magazine *Les Inrockuptibles*. He was asked about several new movies, including Verhoeven's 1997 science-fiction satire *Starship Troopers*, which, unlike its much-abused predecessor, had been something of a critical cause célèbre. Rivette offered a few words of praise for *Starship Troopers*, but he was more expansive in talking about *Showgirls*, which he called "one of the great American films of the last few years." He went on, "It is a movie about surviving in a world populated by assholes, and that's [Verhoeven's] philosophy . . . of all the recent American films that were set in Las Vegas, *Showgirls* was the only one that was real — take my word for it. I, who have never set foot in the place."[10]

"In my films, I hold a mirror up to life," wrote Paul Verhoeven before the release of *Showgirls*.[11] While it is always a risk to take this frequently wiseacre filmmaker at his word, there is something to this assertion. This book contends that *Showgirls* is a movie that is also a mirror, one that offers a vivid rearview on a very particular pop-cultural moment and also a telling reflection of the viewer. This is not to say that *Showgirls* is a Rorschach test. Rorschach diagrams are, by their nature, opaque — black ink splashed against a blank surface, they are designed to elicit a high degree of creative interpretation. *Showgirls*, however, is utterly transparent. Fans and detractors alike see right through it. If the viewer wants to see a "piece of shit," chances are that he will; certainly enough people did and still do. If the viewer knows how to look, however, then *Showgirls*' magnificence will reveal itself as grandly and nakedly as a striptease.

For some, the picture will get clearer with repeated looks, as it did for Jeffrey Sconce, whose contribution to the *Film Quarterly* symposium, entitled "I Have Grown Weary of Your Tiresome Cinema," is an entertaining experiment in relentless re-viewing. "If you see *Showgirls* just once," he writes, "it will linger simply as an exercise in bad excess." Then, later: "Leaving the theater after screening two, one begins to wonder: is the film bad, or just highly, highly stylized? And how would I be able to tell the difference?" Moving along: "At the third screening, Verhoeven's genius is unmistakable . . . it's not bad filmmaking — it's a brilliant savaging of the vapidity of Hollywood's typical narrative machinery."[12] By the end of screening four, Sconce is breathlessly invoking Roland Barthes's "Myth Today" and name-checking Brecht and Baudrillard, declaring that *Showgirls* is nothing less than a "long-lost Edenic text of bliss."

Crucially, Sconce only caught up with *Showgirls* a year

after its initial release, when it had already been branded as a piece of shit. This quality of seeming better in retrospect is not uncommon when it comes to cult movies, be they fortunately rediscovered (*à la* the Coen brothers' sublime yet initially underappreciated *The Big Lebowski* [1998]) or cannily pre-packaged like *The Rocky Horror Picture Show*, a film that fails Sontag's definition of "naïve" or "pure camp" and instead succeeds as a piece of calculated kitsch. *Showgirls* was never supposed to be a cult movie: it was supposed to be a big mainstream hit, and movies playing that sort of high-stakes game seldom get a second chance to make a first impression. And when somebody styles his career like Paul Verhoeven, always trying to be the fly in the ointment, he's begging to get swatted from time to time.

Both Verhoeven and Eszterhas were asking for it around the time of *Showgirls'* release. The people responsible for unleashing *Basic Instinct* on an unsuspecting populace three years earlier were not about to get the benefit of the doubt the next time out. In the month before *Showgirls'* premiere, so much ink was spilled describing which parts of the female anatomy the movie was going to show, there wasn't much left over to print anything but words that were nasty, brutish, and short: "bore" (*New York Times*), "porn" (*Toronto Star"*), "shoddy" (*Village Voice*), "stinkeroo" (*Globe and Mail*).

Showgirls is a movie that deserves to be scrutinized beyond these initial scandalized glances. The fear, though, is that the longer we gaze into this particular abyss, the more we may begin to suspect that it's gawping back at us beneath a pixie-bobbed wig and tacky false eyelashes. But you also don't have to read Lewis Carroll to know that it can be a great adventure to stare at a mirror until you fall through the other side and poke around. That way lies Wonderland. But before we go any further, we need to take a quick look in our rearview mirrors . . .

3

Getting Away with Murder

In the final scene of *Basic Instinct*, San Francisco homicide detective Nick Curran (Michael Douglas) is in bed with Catherine Tramell (Sharon Stone), a bestselling crime novelist whom he has every reason to suspect is also a sociopathic serial killer — knowledge that has not kept him from taking her as his lover. The authorities are convinced that the perp was Nick's other lover, police psychologist Beth Garner (Jeanne Tripplehorn). Momentarily convinced of her guilt by evidence planted by Catherine, Nick had plugged Beth in a hotel hallway with his service revolver and then held her close as she professed her love to him with her dying breath.

Nick has made a lot of dumb mistakes by this point in the story, but he is smarter than the other detectives in his squad. Too late, he realizes that Catherine, a calculating criminal genius whose gory novels offer veiled confessions of her predations, set Beth up. What's more, he understands that by falling into bed with Catherine, he's making himself an accessory after the fact. He's acting like a fool. Whether it's a booty call or a death wish, he's gotta have it.

"What do we do now, Nick?" asks Catherine, her back turned to Nick and her expression concealed from him (and us) by the coy placement of the camera. Nick has an answer at the ready: "Fuck like minks, raise rug rats, and live happily ever after." The desultory tone suggests that not even he believes the words coming out of his mouth. The camera pans down to Catherine's face and then lower, past the bottom of the bed and toward the floor, as she reaches for an unseen object, stopping just short of revealing it.

The camera then travels back upward and catches Catherine's usually placid face in a state of mild distress. "I hate rug rats," she says, almost with a whimper. "Fuck like minks, forget the rug rats, and live happily ever after," replies Nick without missing a beat. They gaze into each other's eyes and Catherine reaches behind her, seemingly for the unseen object. But when her arm comes up her hand is empty. She pulls Nick close as Jerry Goldsmith's score swells romantically around them. The venetian blinds cast serrated shadows on the bed as the pair begin to enact the first phase of Nick's fairy-tale ending. And the camera glides down once more to the floor, this time revealing the ice pick under the bed. It gleams ominously before the final cut to black.

Basic Instinct's final shot is a visual joke on the Sword of

Damocles, the well-honed blade that hangs above the head of every person who desires power and glory, poised to fall at any moment and curtail his ambitions in a single cutting stroke. This is a high-toned allusion, but Nick's predicament also plays slyly on the ending of Douglas's big hit *Fatal Attraction* (1987), the film that initiated the cycle of erotic thrillers that *Basic Instinct* had the final, deeply sarcastic word on. In that film, Douglas's philandering husband is poised to meet his fate at the wrong end of a knife wielded by his spurned lover (Glenn Close), only to be saved at the last moment when his wife (Anne Archer) busts through the bathroom door and shoots the madwoman in the chest, saving her husband's life and her marriage in the bargain. (Or, as Pauline Kael dryly observed, "the family that kills together, stays together."[13]) In *Basic Instinct*, there is no wife or family, and no last-minute rescue: Nick must lie in the cozy deathbed he's made for himself.

That final shot also turns what had previously been an exercise in ambiguity into an open-and-shut case. Without it, there is at least a faint possibility that Catherine Tramell is not a calculating, manipulative serial murderess, but merely a calculating, manipulative professional writer whose intimate connection to a string of grisly killings is simply a matter of coincidence. But the ice pick cannot be a coincidence, not in balmy summertime San Francisco — and certainly not under the bed! This is very bad news for Nick, and yet also very satisfying to the viewer because it imparts a sense of closure. It's now beyond dispute that Catherine Tramell got away with murder. And, given the proximity of her weapon of choice and the nature of her pathology, it's only a matter of time — perhaps even a few minutes — before she does it again.

With *Basic Instinct*, Paul Verhoeven and Joe Eszterhas also got away with murder, even if they bickered all the way to the scene of the crime and left in separate getaway cars. In the late 1980s, the Dutch-born director and the Hungarian émigré screenwriter arguably did more than any other mainstream filmmakers to reshape the Hollywood landscape in their own images: Verhoeven by drizzling blood and gore over the heavy-metal chassis of the '80s-model action movie, Eszterhas by lubricating his high-concept screenplays with a thin, clingy layer of sleaze.

Three years after *The Terminator* (1984) created a fad for monosyllabic killer cyborgs, Verhoeven's *RoboCop* was a game-changer: a science-fiction thriller that torqued the hard-body tendency of American action cinema and drove it to its metallic extreme. Verhoeven, who had never made a movie in America before, had been an unexpected choice for the project, but beyond his skill at bringing an over-budgeted production in at fighting trim, he'd displayed a basic instinct for the workings of genre cinema. A *Dirty Harry* redux in body armor, *RoboCop* boasted grotesque special effects and brutal violence, more than earning its hard-R rating.

Eszterhas, meanwhile, was an eternal adolescent, contentious, idealistic, and shameless. A former investigative journalist, as a screenwriter he quickly became the poster boy for punchy premises — "the Swami of the High Concept," according to Richard Corliss.[14] Holding nothing back,

Eszterhas's screenplays left it all on the floor like Jennifer Beals's Alex auditioning for the starchy culture vultures at the Pittsburgh Conservatory of Dance and Repertory at the end of Eszterhas's first big hit, *Flashdance* (1983). That movie (directed by Adrian Lyne, who would later helm *Fatal Attraction*) had a concept so rigidly and perfectly programmatic — welder by day, exotic dancer by night — that it triumphed over a slate of bad reviews and launched Eszterhas into the Hollywood stratosphere. His script for Richard Marquand's dexterous whodunit *Jagged Edge* (1985) laid the template for the later wave of erotic thrillers, while the more prestigious productions *Music Box* (1989) and *Betrayed* (1988) still managed to trade in sensationalized subject matter — nasty Nazi war criminals and wicked white supremacists respectively.

As the 1990s dawned, both Verhoeven and Eszterhas were at their creative and commercial apex. Verhoeven had his choice of projects after delivering back-to-back hits with *RoboCop* and the Arnold Schwarzenegger sci-fi vehicle *Total Recall*, while Eszterhas was the rare screenwriter who was considered "bankable" in the same manner as a star actor or big-name director. *Basic Instinct*, with its neo-noir cynicism, erotic-thriller gleam and title connoting powerful, irresistible impulses, would be less a joint project than a summit, a public meeting of the (dirty) minds.

Eszterhas had conceived *Basic Instinct* in homage to the films of Alfred Hitchcock, especially *Vertigo* (1958), from which he borrowed the scenic San Francisco backdrop. The director was a favorite of Verhoeven's as well: *The Fourth*

Man (1983) was basically a full-dress tribute to the Master of Suspense, right down to co-star Renée Soutendijk's icy-blonde temptress. What was really startling, however — indeed, bordering on the uncanny — was how closely *Basic Instinct* resembled *The Fourth Man*: both were stories of addled, addicted men in thrall to voracious blondes with hidden agendas and strings of literal skeletons hanging in their closets, and both ended with their horndog semi-heroes hoisted with their own kinky petards.

Verhoeven and Eszterhas may have been on the same Hitchcockian wavelength, but they could also barely stand to be in the same room together. Carolco Pictures, the upstart independent production company that shelled out the then-record amount of $3 million for Eszterhas's script in 1991, thought that it was protecting its investment by hiring Verhoeven, but Eszterhas wasn't impressed. The writer had been hoping instead for the Oscar-winning Czech director Miloš Forman, whose pedigree, including *One Flew Over the Cuckoo's Nest* (1975) and *Amadeus* (1984), was considerably classier than that of the Dutch provocateur.[15]

Eszterhas's bitterness increased when he and Verhoeven started arguing over the script, with the director insisting that the writer add a lesbian sex scene. Suddenly, the guy who'd happily signed his name to a movie about a gyrating 18-year-old sexpot with a blowtorch and a crazy dream was put in the position of being both the resident prude and the voice of restraint. The famously combative Verhoeven expected to roll right over his collaborator. "Look, I am the director, *ja*?

And you are the writer. So I am right and you are wrong, *ja*?" he reportedly screamed during their first meeting. Eszterhas didn't back down: "And me saying to Paul: If you use that tone of voice with me again, I'm going to come across the fucking table at you!"[16]

The two remained at odds throughout *Basic Instinct*'s production, which was marred by protests by gay rights groups who had gotten a hold of the script and blanched at its apparent portrayal of bisexual women as sociopathic man-killers. That the film was being shot in San Francisco, the most famously queer-positive city in the United States and the site of several milestones in the history of LGBT activism, added insult to injury. Verhoeven ended up defending the screenplay against representatives of the gay community and also Eszterhas himself, who walked off the production in the wake of the complaints.[17]

Basic Instinct was submitted to the MPAA seven times just to receive an R rating in lieu of an NC-17. Even with the trims, the sequence in which Catherine Tramell uncrosses her legs and flashes her vagina at a group of hardened cops during a police investigation became an instant conversation piece. It was also an emblem of Verhoeven's by now infamous anything-goes mentality: Sharon Stone claimed that Verhoeven gotten the shot on the sly after lying to her that the set would be darkened to reduce visibility. The actress was furious when she saw the completed scene, and so was everybody else. The film was picketed by protestors and pilloried by critics, including the *Globe and Mail*'s Jay Scott, who wrote that

"Everyone associated with *Basic Instinct* should be spanked and sent to bed without supper, but on the basis of the evidence at hand in this sadomasochistic disaster, they might enjoy it."[18]

4

The Verhoeven Touch

Scott might have been right about Verhoeven, who had been gleefully making people uncomfortable for years. If the Dutch director was an auteur, then he was a provoc-auteur — a filmmaker who went out of his way to shock his audience. Born in 1938 in Amsterdam, Verhoeven was a brainy kid and an authentic polymath: he attended the Leiden University for degrees in mathematics and physics before switching to film school, where he quickly became impatient. "We all had to make Dutch realism: windmills, clay, potatoes, lots of dikes, and so on. I quit the course early in the second year, because I had the feeling that I wasn't learning anything."[19] Verhoeven dropped out of the program and then slagged his alma matter from the winner's podium at a student film festival.

This moment would prove prophetic. Though Dutch

cinema had been primarily associated with documentary filmmaking in the years after World War II, like many other young European directors of the period Verhoeven practiced his cinephilia devoutly; he had an especial appreciation for the literate and boldly stylized works of David Lean, Laurence Olivier, and Alfred Hitchcock. Verhoeven's reverence for film history was balanced against his irreverence toward virtually everything else. Emerging out of a culture that valued tolerance and self-effacement, he was an institutional irritant, *enfant terrible*, and one-man "new wave" in the making.

The tragicomic romance *Turkish Delight* (1973) — starring future *Blade Runner* replicant Rutger Hauer as an uninhibited artist who claims that he "fucks better than God," and takes every opportunity to prove his boast — was Verhoeven's first great success, quickly becoming the most popular Dutch film ever made and only the third to be nominated for an Academy Award. *Katie Tippel* (1975), a 19th-century picaresque about a blonde social-climber, and the World War II resistance epic *Soldier of Orange* (1977) were similarly well-received, despite many controversial elements. It was with *Spetters* (1980) — a lusty drama about a trio of feckless, motocross-loving youths who spend their nights drinking, cursing, carousing, and chasing girls through a dilapidated rural Dutch landscape — that Verhoeven finally got himself into serious trouble. The film's calculated provocations — most notably a mid-movie homosexual gang-rape sequence — caused a genuine scandal, so much so that a group calling itself the Nederlandse Anti-*Spetters* Actie (Dutch Anti-*Spetters* Action) began campaigning for a boycott in the weeks after the film's release, distributing leaflets warning that it would "reinforce existing prejudices about women, homosexuals, and other minority groups."[20]

Sympathetic reviewers, however, understood that the film's outrageousness was a deliberate strategy. Though Verhoeven's "spetters" (an outdated term that translates roughly in English to "hunks") were recognizable Dutch cousins to the Wild Ones and Rebels without Causes who'd blazed their way through 1950s Hollywood cinema, what made the movie so unsettling was how it identified with its sexually and economically frustrated protagonists' impulses to pillage, ravage, and destroy, without condoning them. In lieu of producing either a stolid social commentary or a gleefully hedonistic joyride, Verhoeven did both at once.

Verhoeven also had it both ways in *The Fourth Man*, which freely adapted Gerard Reve's novel about an alcoholic novelist (Jeroen Krabbé) ensnared by a beautiful admirer (Renée Soutendijk) who beds him on a book tour. The film was a high-toned thriller so jam-packed with portentous symbols — creeping spiders, looming crucifixes, and a red scarf that always appears as a prelude to a murder — that film critics found themselves in a quandary. Previously, reviewers had carped that the lone superstar of Dutch cinema had spent his time and his talent and government subsidies making disreputable trash rather than art. *The Fourth Man*, though, had so many arty touches that it had to be taken seriously.

Or did it? "It was widely assumed that *The Fourth Man* . . . was satirical, but I remember standing in the lobby of a Toronto theater when [it] received its premiere courtesy of the Festival of Festivals," recalled Jay Scott in his pan of *Basic Instinct*. "[Verhoeven] was furious that the audience was laughing. Later, when he realized that the film was a hit for whatever reason, he started telling interviewers that Toronto audiences were the first to understand that he had made a comedy. How do you define Opportunist?"[21] Yet Kevin Courrier, a Toronto-based author and film critic, remembers the festival screening differently. He also bumped into Verhoeven in the theater hallway afterward, where the director, sensing that he was in the presence of a roomful of satisfied customers, smiled maliciously and asked, "Pretty good, no?" Courrier says that he couldn't do much but nod in agreement.

These brazen tendencies did not recede when, a few years later, Verhoeven arrived in America following his last hometown hurrah with *The Fourth Man*. The director was excited at the opportunity to work in a more permissive cultural environment and with greater financial resources. As opposed to the juvenilia of *Star Wars* or the Wagnerian pomp of *Blade Runner*, *RoboCop* employed its sci-fi setting to revel in unabashedly orgiastic bloodletting; Verhoeven contrived scenes of almost whimsical brutality, as when an unlucky junior executive at a weapons-development firm is shot to pieces by a malfunctioning "peacekeeping" drone in the very first sequence.

Total Recall saw *RoboCop*'s body count and raised it, setting new standards for violence in a mainstream American movie while finding ways to keep the viewer from becoming comfortably numb. Having a combatant use another person as a human shield during a firefight is one thing; making the shield in question an innocent bystander, and then pointedly inserting a shot of his bloodied corpse being heedlessly trampled by the bad guys as they continue their pursuit, is what we might call the Verhoeven Touch.

Given Verhoeven's track record, nobody should have been blindsided by *Basic Instinct*'s nasty tone and graphic content. Once again, the combative filmmaker was throwing his punches in crafty combination. The Hitchcockian allusions — the crisp widescreen photography, the Bernard Hermann-esque score, the icy-blonde object of desire — were the setup jabs; the haymakers, meanwhile, were landed mostly below the belt. When Catherine Tramell uncrosses her legs, it at once embodies and obliterates the subtext of the entire scene (and the entire movie) up to that point. The character's smirking and ultimately ruthless lack of subtlety or discretion was perfectly in sync with the filmmaker's; the director and his femme fatale both knew exactly what they were doing, even if the actress in between them was momentarily left out of the loop.

Even the man who wrote the scene in the first place felt like he'd been sucker-punched. After *Basic Instinct*'s premiere, Eszterhas had to admit to his 16-year-old son that the panties-free staging of the sequence hadn't been his idea. That moment of fatherly embarrassment, combined with the fact that *Basic Instinct* grossed $352 million worldwide, convinced him that maybe Verhoeven had known what he was doing all along. In fall 1992, Eszterhas cinched another multimillion-dollar writing contract by pitching high-rolling producer Charles

Evans on a movie that would be the "end-all account of lap dancers and topless performers on the fabled Las Vegas Strip." And his first choice for a director this time would not be Milos Forman. Who needed a two-time Oscar winner when you could get the Verhoeven Touch?

Verhoeven and Eszterhas famously patched things up at a dinner at the elegant Ivy Restaurant in Beverly Hills. "Joe was gracious enough to admit that I had been correct to ignore the pressure groups and to make the film the way he wrote it," wrote Verhoeven in the introduction to *Showgirls: Portrait of a Film*, a glossy book of erotic photographs commissioned for the film's release.[22] (Reading this lovingly produced tome now is a bit like flipping through a vintage press kit for the *Titanic*.) "We had a few drinks, a few laughs, rediscovered our friendship and began to discuss the possibility of doing another project together . . . during an hour or so, [we] talked about dozens of movie ideas . . . Joe was the one who proposed, 'What about a musical about Las Vegas?' I was hooked immediately. Joe claims that my eyes began to glisten."[23]

It must have been a fun lunch: in *The Devil's Guide to Hollywood*, Eszterhas claims that his first draft of his script was "scrawled over with [Verhoeven's] pencil drawings of the way he saw the scene onscreen. Paul's script is an erotic comic book of breasts, butts, and vaginas, accompanied by my words translated into Paul's Dutch."[24] A potential hit was on the table, along with visions of happily-ever-after. But the two still had blood on their hands from *Basic Instinct*, and it can be hard to outrun your sordid past. Just ask Nomi Malone.

5

"You Got a Name?"

Showgirls begins with Nomi entering frame right, walking briskly through a roadside parking lot. We follow her as she turns to approach the highway, where she stops beside a sign reading "Las Vegas 342" and jerks a thumb in the direction of oncoming traffic. A few moments later, a blue pick-up truck arrives, trailing honky-tonk music through its windows. "Where are you going?" she asks the driver (Dewey Weber), a youngish good old boy with an Elvis Presley pompadour and a Jack Nicholson grin. "Vegas," he answers. "Come on, this is your lucky day." She hops in and they peel rubber down the road.

It has been said that there are exactly two plots in all of fiction: a stranger comes to town, or somebody goes on a journey. Within the first ten minutes of *Showgirls*, Nomi will take a crack at both of them. At this early juncture, there are actually two travelers, and two strangers — the other being Jeff, the driver, who looks and sounds like bad news. "You can sit a little bit closer if you want," he drawls, motioning to a spot at his side. Nomi produces a switchblade and unfurls it in his direction: "Back off, motherfucker." "I sure am glad you're going to be such good company," says Jeff, just before Nomi changes the station by stabbing it with her knife. Jeff looks like he's worried about what he's gotten himself in for. Viewers might be thinking the same thing.

At this point, just two minutes into *Showgirls*, it is not too early to consider very seriously what we think of Nomi, and to think about what kind of company she's going to be for the rest of the movie. Jeff makes noises about dumping her at the side of the road, but he relents when she puts the blade away. Realizing that he's not about to get lucky, he settles for making small talk. "You got a name?" he asks. Our heroine hesitates and replies, "Nomi."

As many critics have remarked, "Nomi" sounds like either "know me" or "no me" — the first inviting recognition ("Know me?"), the second a suggestion of blankness. A third possibility is that the emphasis should really be on the second syllable, as in "no . . . *me*," an appropriately self-aggrandizing attitude for a young woman with visions of stardom flash-dancing in her head.

This bit of cryptic etymology gives us our first opportunity to test the theory that *Showgirls* is a two-way mirror — that it's only as great or as terrible as the viewer desires it to be. If Eszterhas's name games strike you as poetic, you should consider yourself attuned to the movie's frequency. If you think it's all just so much pretentious wordplay, you're in for as long and enervating a ride as Jeff. But either way, we have to acknowledge that a deliberate choice as been made about the character's name, and that if we follow that logic through the rest of the movie, it is possible to parse *Showgirls* in terms of its creators' intentions. Instead of treating each memorable moment as a fluke or an accident, we can conclude that, for better or for worse, it's supposed to be there. The question is what do we do with it?

The next item on the docket is Elizabeth Berkley. If we take Nomi's name to be a question mark — "Know me?" — then we might say that it applies as much to the actress as to the character. In 1995, a large segment of the moviegoing audience would have definitely known Berkley, although its members could not legally purchase a ticket for *Showgirls*. To preteens of the early '90s, Berkley was Jessie Spano, the straight-A/Type-A class president on NBC's Saturday-morning sitcom *Saved by the Bell* (1989–1993), a small-screen riff on *Ferris Bueller's Day Off* (1986) that capitalized on the late-'80s vogue for smart-talking, self-aware high-school comedies.

Berkley had actually auditioned for the sitcom's lead role of head cheerleader Kelly Kapowski, but after Tiffani-Amber Thiessen got the part, the show's writers devised a whole new main character just to keep Berkley around. On a show that often went for the goofiest joke possible, the 17-year-old actress was the closest thing in the cast to a straight man.

Berkley's Jessie was often the voice of reason in her relationship with meatheaded wrestler A.C. Slater (Mario Lopez) and chided her best friend Zack (Mark-Paul Gosselaar) for his various zany schemes. It was in many ways a thankless role, but Berkley, who had trained as a dancer as a child and modeled as a teenager, held the camera more naturally than most of her co-stars. She also did more of the heavy dramatic lifting, as in the second-season episode "Jessie's Song," where Jessie, stressing over a college education, gets addicted to caffeine pills and suffers a nervous breakdown.

Search for "Jessie Spano Caffeine Pill Freakout" on YouTube and you'll find a clip with nearly 2 million views and nearly 3,000 comments, most of which are decidedly uncomplimentary. Discovered by Zack in her bedroom, in the middle of a manic episode, Jessie strenuously denies that anything is wrong and breaks into an a cappella rendition of the Pointer Sisters' "I'm So Excited" before eventually dissolving into sobs. "I'm so excited . . . I'm so excited . . . I'm so scared," she wails as Zack embraces her and the commercial break arrives to give the audience time to process the seriousness of this Very Special Episode.

To Berkley's credit, it's hard to imagine any other member of the *Saved by the Bell* cast even attempting that sort of acting. But even if she had more gravitas than Tiffani-Amber Thiessen or Lark Voorhies, it's not as if Berkley created the sort of shaded, nuanced character that Clare Danes did on *My So-Called Life* (1994–1995) or Michelle Williams did on *Dawson's Creek* (1998–2003), shows that departed from the frivolous tone of

Saved by the Bell. Given the generally lightweight nature of her performances, it begs the question of why Paul Verhoeven, who had carte blanche to cast anybody he liked in his new movie, would settle on the erstwhile Ms. Spano.

It's easy enough to see why Berkley went for it, however. Nomi is a classic ingénue — a young, inexperienced performer hoping to make her name in a town not known for being kind to such naïve creatures. In her own mind, she has the talent and the tenacity to succeed, and she's driven by the desire to start over, to ditch an embarrassing backstory and rewrite her life story in a more triumphant vein. She expects to conquer show business on her own terms, and she denies the possibility that all she's really doing is getting in line to be exploited. Reading the script, Elizabeth Berkley might have felt like she was looking in a mirror.

She surely wasn't shy about making her desire for the part known. The story goes that Berkley called producer Charles Evans and introduced herself over the phone as "Nomi from *Showgirls*," and later strode into Verhoeven's office insisting that there was nobody else who could possibly play the role.[25] "I trust Paul completely" is what she said when asked how she felt about doing so many nude scenes.[26] On the set, the director made a show of getting chummy and borderline intimate with his star. In set reports, a Svengali-ish dynamic emerged: "A patient mentor, [Verhoeven] explains what he intends to do with the scene, and is not ashamed to whisper words of encouragement into the actress' ear. He caresses and embraces her, cracks jokes with her — all of which is intended to put Elizabeth, his material, at her ease."[27] It sounds as if Berkley was putty in her director's hands, a statuesque slab of clay awaiting the Verhoeven Touch.

Berkley sincerely believed that *Showgirls* could make her a star. In an article published in *Premiere* in 1995, she remembered filming the scene where Nomi auditions at the Stardust and mentally rewriting one of the posters on the set from "Cristal Connors is a Goddess" to "Elizabeth Berkley starring in *Showgirls*." "It was *so* emotional" is how Berkley put it.[28] The same can be said of her acting. Of all the things critics accused Berkley of in their reviews of *Showgirls*, reticence was not one of them. Right from the first scene, she seems to be bristling against every other element of the production: she stares daggers at her co-star, spits out her dialogue like it's trying to poison her, and manhandles any and all props that she gets her fabulously manicured hands on.

If we compare Berkley's frantic acting to Sharon Stone's icily precise work in *Basic Instinct*, a number of contrasts emerge. Sharon Stone the actress and Catherine Tramell the character both give the impression that they know exactly what they're doing; Elizabeth Berkley and Nomi Malone do not. This could simply be a case of one woman being a better or more experienced actress than the other, but even though Stone was a decade older when she made *Basic Instinct* than Berkley circa *Showgirls*, she was hardly a seasoned veteran or an established star. What she did was play the role of a distaff devil fully to the hilt. Everything in *Basic Instinct* is calibrated to emphasize Catherine's seductive beauty and sadistic brilliance.

The same cannot be said of *Showgirls*, which has a different kind of ambivalence toward its female protagonist. Catherine Tramell is a mystery woman who really isn't that mysterious — it's simply a matter of how long it's going to take Nick Curran to catch on to something the audience has suspected all along. She's also a cool customer with wealth and status on her side, taunting the working stiffs on the police force from her beachfront living room. Nomi, on the other hand, is a desperate woman (a bit like the hustler Stone played in Martin Scorsese's *Casino* [1995]) and her confusion from moment to moment is palpable. Nomi's defense mechanisms are less developed than Catherine's: she doesn't draw others in so much as hold them at arm's length, with a switchblade in hand. Jeff looks tempted to just dump her by the side of the road, but he doesn't. He's stuck with her, and so are we.

Next stop, Las Vegas.

6

"Ain't Anybody Ever Been Nice to You?"

Nomi Malone isn't the first shady lady to set out for Sin City: in 1952's *The Las Vegas Story*, a blowsy ex-lounge singer played by Jane Russell gets dragged back to the Nevadan hotspot by new husband Vincent Price only to encounter a beefy ex-flame (Victor Mature). Laid out end to end, the titles of the films set in the neon oasis tell a florid story of love gone wrong: *Meet Me in Las Vegas* (1956), *Honeymoon in Vegas* (1992), *Fear and Loathing in Las Vegas* (1998), *Leaving Las Vegas* (1995). A city of midnight runs and indecent proposals, the primo destination for those looking to get Lost in America — from the road-tripping Griswold clan in *Vegas Vacation* (1997) to the overgrown frat boys of *The Hangover* (2009) — Las Vegas has been one of the most frequently filmed cities in the history of American movies, and like Los Angeles, its geography is such that it can only play itself. Nobody is going to mistake a shot of the Strip for any-where else. And yet Las Vegas is a city with a split personality. It's paradise for the winners and purgatory for everyone else. It's the opposite of the Hotel California: you can leave any time you like, but only after you've made the check out.

The first image of Las Vegas in *Showgirls* is rather unin-spiring. Over Jeff's shoulder, we see a line of blinking towers, their light-up signs just far enough away that we can't quite make out the words. "Do you gamble?" Jeff asks Nomi, flashing that good old-boy grin. When she answers in the negative, he tells her, "You've gotta gamble if you're going to win." "I'm going to win," she says, but the remark seems directed inward, as if she's trying to convince herself more than her chauffeur. The truck cruises lazily in to the Riviera casino's parking lot, in effect returning Nomi to the same sort of empty, liminal space that she started from — an indicator, perhaps, that on this journey she will be fated to keep returning to square one.

En route to Las Vegas, Nomi seemed naïve about her prospects, but her wariness was an effective defense mecha-nism. Now that she's actually made it there, she drops her guard enough that even a transparent huckster like Jeff can get the better of her. He convinces Nomi to leave her suitcase in the car while he fetches his uncle, who he claims has job con-nections at the casino. "Ain't anybody ever been nice to you?" he asks, knowing full well that the answer is no and that he's not about to be the first.

In *Showgirls: Portrait of a Film*, Paul Verhoeven writes that he and his cinematographer, Jost Vacano, were aiming for a "very free, fluid look," which entailed the use of the Steadicam, a stabilizing camera mount that isolates the camera from the movement of the operator.[29] An invention of the American cinematographer Garrett Brown, the Steadicam came into vogue in the late 1970s, as it allowed directors to choreograph elaborate tracking shots that could glide through sets and locations without betraying any of the bumpiness or shakiness of traditional handheld camerawork. In *The Shining*, Stanley Kubrick exploited the Steadicam's visual possibilities to the fullest, prowling through the corridors of the haunted Overlook Hotel with the eerie serenity of a floating ghost.

The Steadicam is first used in *Showgirls* when Nomi and Jeff go into the Riviera and he leaves her to wander the slot machines, handing her a ten-dollar bill for walking-around money, which she snatches from him like a mongoose trying to kill a cobra. The shot isn't as spectacular as the signature sequence of Martin Scorsese's *Goodfellas* (1990), which descends into the bowels of a New Jersey nightclub in a single fluid take, but it does give us enough time to drink in the setting and to register that the actors are not on a movie set. Verhoeven believes that the Steadicam can impart a documentary quality to a fictional film: "On the screen, it appears as though the camera is following the actors, as it might do in cinéma verité . . . basically, you never see the camera moving without being motivated by an actor, but I have choreographed the actor so that the camera can find a new angle."[30]

Even if we don't accept Verhoeven's aspirations to "realism" here, we can still see a clear attempt on behalf of the director to undermine the fantasy of Las Vegas that he (and Nomi) has to this point been building up. Like any rude awakening, this jolt is presaged by an almost dreamlike serenity, as Nomi pulls the lever on the first slot machine and is rewarded with a steady stream of coins. But she doesn't quit while she's ahead, and in the space between two cuts, she's back down to zero — and also to the violent, impulsive gestures of her initial appearance, as she punches the machine in rage and frustration.

Like a shark sniffing blood in the water, a man cruises by and propositions Nomi, telling her that he has some ideas about how she can make her money back. "Sooner or later, you're going to have to sell it," he calls as she strides away, seething. Losing the money is a wake-up call for Nomi that nothing in Las Vegas is going to be as easy as it seems, that the town's M.O. is to give you little glimpses of victory before snatching them away. We won't know just how deeply Nomi is stung by the catcaller's insinuation until much later in the movie, but we've definitely seen enough, even in this one brief encounter, to validate Jacques Rivette's claims that *Showgirls* is "about surviving in a world populated by assholes" — not only this guy, with his slick haircut and shirt unbuttoned to reveal a cheap gold chain, but also Jeff, who has swiftly and predictably made off with Nomi's suitcase for the low price of ten bucks.

Running out to the parking lot, Nomi realizes she's been had. With no slot machine around to punch, she starts thrashing the hood of a nearby car, which prompts its owner, Molly (Gina Ravera), to rush over and stop her. She grabs Nomi, who breaks away and vomits on the ground, then nearly gets creamed lurching out into the middle of the road. Spent and broke, Nomi falls into Molly's arms and begins weeping uncontrollably.

Molly, as it turns out, is the answer to Jeff's question about whether anyone's ever been nice to Nomi. In the very next scene, she sits her down at a fast food restaurant and treats her to some French fries and a soft drink. Nomi is still agitated, however: she files her nails like she's power-sanding a porch swing and stabs a straw into the top of her drink as if to draw blood. She can't even pour ketchup on her food without sending the stuff flying into the air like a squib exploding in *RoboCop*. She doesn't want to answer Molly's questions about her past, or her family, or where she's from. But the other woman has a soft, calming presence, and she surprises Nomi by asking her if she'd like to crash at her place for a few days. "Are you hitting on me?" asks Nomi, smiling as if to indicate that this wouldn't be the worst thing in the world. "No," says Molly just as coyly, wrapping her lips around her own straw and taking a pull off her Coke.

Is she hitting on her? The Molly-Nomi pairing is, if not the most important relationship in *Showgirls*, then certainly the most tender. Molly remains a steadfast friend throughout the story, and in the end she's the one person who Nomi proves (literally) willing to fight for. Their ensuing trailer park cohabitation, while not explicitly sexual, is undoubtedly cozy: Molly isn't shy about dressing and undressing in front of her new roommate, and Nomi looks pretty comfortable leaning across Molly's body to grab the television remote.

"When the filmmakers imagine domestic life between Nomi and Molly," wrote Janet Maslin in the *New York Times*, "they see chicks in lingerie who giggle, clutch stuffed animals, fuss about manicures, and say 'What am I going to wear?' and 'Who ate the chips?'"[31] Maslin is not wrong about the sneakily prurient vibe of the trailer-park scenes, although she misses the genuine affection between the characters, feelings that rarely permeate any of the movie's other interactions. Nomi and Molly aren't in love, but they seem to love each other; and in a movie that is in all other respects violently allergic to subtlety of any kind, the affectionate ambiguity of their relationship definitely stands out.

So too does the color of Molly's skin. Molly is black, and while this fact is never explicitly remarked upon by anybody in the film, it's hardly a case of color-blind casting. Chon Noriega believes that Molly and another key supporting character — Glenn Plummer's James — "represent Hollywood's usual nonwhite Good Samaritans," and points out that all the black characters in the film "occupy subservient roles: seamstress, bouncer, bellhop, bodyguard, attendant."[32] Noriega is not claiming that Verhoeven and Eszterhas are racist, but that by aligning Nomi and Molly, the filmmakers are placing them on a shared continuum — not only on a plane of female friendship apart from the competitive power-gaming that will define Nomi's love/hate affair with Cristal Connors, but also as second-tier citizens within Las Vegas's social and professional hierarchy.

If we give Molly the same benefit of the doubt, maybe she's being nice to Nomi not because she wants something from her, but because she recognizes another girl who's down on her luck. The difference is that while Molly will be content to indefinitely extend her trailer-park idyll, Nomi is intent on integrating more fully into the "world of assholes" and, if necessary, becoming one herself. She gets her chance when Molly implores her to visit the Stardust, where she works as a seamstress. It's an invitation to a cutthroat world, and as if to emphasize this point, Verhoeven includes a close-up of Nomi's nails, which she's painted in a pink-and-purple snakeskin pattern that make them look like day-glo claws — Freddy Krueger after a Saturday morning at the salon. "They'll all be so jealous," purrs Molly. She's referring to her friend's manicure, but her words are also very prescient about the backstage of the Stardust in general, a sweaty tangle of thin skins and easily bruised egos.

"All right, you guys, let's go, let's do this," barks Dee (Bobbie Phillips), the de facto major-domo of the Stardust dance troupe. It's two minutes to show time and the show-girls are a mess. Molly's job is doing triage on frayed costumes, but our focus is on Nomi — not only because of her hot pink dress, but because her gaping confusion at the swirl of activity around her mirrors our own. The return of the Steadicam plunges us back into something that looks like a real space, with bodies bustling across the frame in every direction. The fact that most of these bodies are nubile and naked (men as well as women) doesn't really make the scene titillating, however. We're just watching people at work, and the catty comments they hiss at each other could just as easily be exchanged at a water cooler as at a dressing table.

Nomi (and the camera) shifts her attention to the big dressing room off to the side, where she (and the audience/ viewer) catches sight of the lean, muscled back of Cristal Connors, nude from the waist up, as she directs a stagehand on where to place her latest congratulatory bouquet. Nomi, momentarily distracted, can barely keep up with the dancers as they run to take their places at the bottom of the stairway leading up to the Stardust's stage, a fateful place that will come to figure significantly in the movie's plot. As the showgirls charge up to the stage en masse, Nomi is shooed up a second flight of stairs where she can watch the show from the balcony. She emerges into the theater as the music swells, framed against the explosions of light and color emanating from the stage below.

The "Goddess" number that follows is a small masterpiece of tackiness. To the pulsating sounds of a rhythm track written by Eurythmics' Dave Stewart, the male and female members of the hotel's ensemble boogie communally around the base of a papier-mâché volcano, which erupts to reveal Cristal in a G-string, writhing sensually amidst puffs of dry ice. Her presence compels the other dancers to ritualistically doff their clothes, as if her "Goddess" were some hybrid incarnation of divine inspiration and original sin. The dancing that follows is impressively athletic, if mechanized, with Cristal being passed between the male dancers like a hot potato. "I think it's the best show I've ever been involved in," says Cristal later, basking in the approbation of her fans and the motley crew of television journalists who've been dispatched to the

"Goddess" premiere. Nomi, who has lingered backstage, watches her charm the reporters with practiced finesse.

During the "Goddess" number, Nomi had eyed the stage intently as if imagining herself in Cristal's place, and it's clear from the faraway look in her eyes that she's still fantasizing now. (The character's name offers a further hint in this direction, crystal being a surface that reflects.) Verhoeven draws the first of many visual parallels between the two characters by framing them each in separate shots in front of a strange gargoyle prop that hovers over their shoulders like an apparition, a loaded bit of set dressing that blends together with the red-hued lighting to suggest a Stygian environment.

Cristal is this underworld's reigning queen, and she's an imposing monarch. Swathed in feathers and bejeweled from head to toe, she's effortlessly yet aggressively glamorous. But she's also vulnerable; at one point, a reporter asks Cristal her age, and she notably declines to answer. Gina Gershon, a Los Angeles–born stage actress who co-founded the New York City theater troupe Naked Angels in 1986, was 32 when she was cast as the 25-year-old Cristal, a decade older than Elizabeth Berkley but just as much of an unknown. In the early '80s, Gershon had appeared as an uncredited dancer in the musicals *Beatlemania* (1981) and *Girls Just Want to Have Fun* (1985), and scored eye-candy supporting roles in *Red Heat* (1988) and *Cocktail* (1988). She was cast in the then white-hot Spike Lee's controversial *Jungle Fever* (1991), but her scenes were deleted. Getting cast in *Showgirls* was as much Gershon's big break as it was Berkley's. However, where the younger actress can barely keep her head above water, Gershon brings to mind that old line about actresses being like swans, giving an appearance of serenity without showing how hard they're paddling underneath the surface.

If Cristal is a swan, though, she's a black one: there's an undercurrent of hostility in everything she does, including brushing by Nomi in the hallway and scratching her with yet another bouquet of roses. Nomi isn't offended by this thorny close encounter — she's elated. Before the film's release, Verhoeven admitted that *Showgirls* was in many ways reminiscent of Joseph L. Mankiewicz's Academy Award–winning classic *All About Eve* (1950), which concerns the rivalry between the aging Broadway star Margo Channing (Bette Davis) and Eve Harrington (Anne Baxter), an adoring young fan who insinuates herself into her idol's life and eventually ends up taking her place. "I call this one *All About Evil*," Verhoeven joked, playing up the narrative resemblance between the two films.[33] There's definitely a hint of Davis's Margo in Gershon's work as Cristal, a cunning malevolence that both the actress and the character use as a reflexive defense mechanism against their surroundings.

The difference is that in *All About Eve*, Davis didn't have to approximate the bearing of a fading titan since she truly was one herself. *All About Eve* marked the midpoint between the actress's 1940s heyday and her gargoyle-like turn in Robert Aldrich's *What Ever Happened to Baby Jane?* (1962). Gershon can't play off her iconography in the same way, because she doesn't have any. Instead, she creates a stylized caricature of a woman who has become a showbiz lifer before her time, who knows exactly what to play up (her flirty Texas twang) and play down (her bitterness and weariness) depending on who is the room.

When Nomi comes to call on Cristal in her dressing room with Molly (who is there to deal with a wardrobe malfunction), Gershon and Cristal push their respective performances into overdrive. Noticing Nomi staring at her in her massive mirror, Cristal takes her hands from her breasts and slides them down to her sides, and the shot is framed in the reflective surface so that we can see Nomi's reaction — startled and turned on — before she looks down at the floor. Molly introduces Nomi to Cristal as a fellow dancer, and Cristal disingenuously asks Nomi where she works. (Her tone implies that she has a pretty good guess.) When Nomi replies that she dances at a club called the Cheetah, Cristal, who has been methodically applying lotion to her face the entire time, replies with calculated coldness: "If it's at the Cheetah, it's not dancing. I know that much."

This is Nomi's cue to exit in a huff, slamming the door with gusto on the way out. She's mortified at the suggestion that her bump-and-grind day job makes her any less of a performer than Cristal, even if she secretly suspects that it's true. To this point in the film, Nomi has defined herself and her mission in Las Vegas as being all about her craft. Cristal's insinuation that she's somehow working to the side of her stated vocation has clearly gotten under her skin. She's so upset, in fact, that the only thing that can possibly cheer her up is hitting the dance floor.

7

"She Can Dance, Can't She?"

The camera floats across the Crave Club before coming to rest on Nomi, still in that hot pink dress, swiveling with extreme prejudice to the sounds of a generic rock track. It is, to say the least, a mesmerizing spectacle. As Eric Schaefer writes, "[Nomi] is revealed at the center of the throng, moving as spastically as a rag doll in a hurricane . . . most viewers will most likely be reminded of Elaine's clueless 'dancing' on *Seinfeld*."[34] There is no evidence that Julia Louis-Dreyfus's priceless "full-body dry heave set to music" was an homage to *Showgirls*, but the comparison is apt, especially since neither woman has any idea of how ridiculous she looks.

If Nomi's aspiration is to dance for a living, it's important that we see what sort of moves she's working with. This was also the case in *Flashdance*, although that movie provided built-in validation for Jennifer Beals's talents in the form of the stuffy conservatory judges, who are initially dubious at her appearance but eventually won over by the athleticism and exuberance of her audition. Every scene in *Flashdance* is pitched to make us think that Alex could be a great dancer if only she could dump her tawdry night job at the cabaret and the class-based feelings of inadequacy that come with it. In *Showgirls*, however, the doubts belong to the characters around Nomi — not only Cristal, whose withering assessment of Nomi's job seems a mixture of seen-it-all wisdom and fierce territoriality, but also amateur choreographer James, whom the film introduces at this moment as a bemused witness to the tasseled pink vortex that is our heroine. "She can dance, can't she?" asks James's friend admiringly. "She thinks she can," answers James with a smirk.

Like Molly, James is almost instantly drawn to Nomi, and, like Molly, he is African-American — an artistic decision that, once again, deserves some scrutiny. James is positioned in the film as Nomi's first (legitimate) male suitor, and the fact that he's black gives their potential coupling a decisively taboo-courting charge. James is also quickly identified as a character with a certain amount of wisdom when it comes to dancing, and also about the workaday (bump and) grind of Las Vegas, slipping a little too easily into the role of the savvy or street-smart black friend familiar from so many Hollywood movies. Sauntering up to Nomi on the dance floor, James tells her that he thinks she has "potential" and offers to teach her some new steps, which could just as easily be seen as a pick-up ploy as a genuine attempt at mentorship. He's also not particularly nice about it, explaining that what Nomi's doing as she gyrates away isn't dancing so much as "teasing [his] dick."

When Cristal said basically the same thing one scene earlier, Nomi fled in shame. Now, out on the dance floor, she feels empowered to respond to this criticism by gracefully pirouetting around and kneeing her new partner in the groin, not "teasing his dick" but pummeling it. James falls into another dancer, setting off a mini-riot that results in both he and Nomi getting hauled off to the police station. Note the title of the song employed to underscore this chaotic passage, in which a provocatively dressed young woman reduces a roomful of grown men to panting, sucker-punching morons just by moving her body in the right way: "I'm Afraid of Americans." One hopes that David Bowie appreciated the joke as much as the money he doubtless received for licensing the track.

"My head hurts, my dick hurts, and I got fired from my job," moans James as he bails Nomi out of lockup. "Shit happens" is her response as she strides in the other direction, James trailing behind. Though cast at least partially because of his skills as a dancer, Glenn Plummer is also a fine, relaxed actor who finds just the right note of perplexity for a man who can't quite understand why he keeps pursuing a woman whose idea of small talk is "Back off, motherfucker," and who responds to his invitation for a cup of coffee by throwing a quarter at him before peeling away in Molly's car to her shift at the Cheetah. Men who don't learn their lesson with regard to blonde objects of desire are recurring figures in the cinema of Paul Verhoeven.

In interviews, Verhoeven made a point of explaining how he, Eszterhas, and producer Ben Myron had done a lot of preliminary research to get a sense of Las Vegas as a city. What they found was a place trying to decide on the right profile to present to the world: a fresh, cleanly scrubbed glamour shot, or a dimly lit late-night come-hither grin. "In the new, 'family-oriented Vegas,' there are still a few shows that feature the real, old-fashioned showgirls with their featured costumes," wrote Verhoeven. "A couple of others, however, such as 'Splash' and 'Into the Night' feature topless nudity and sexy dancing, and this was much closer to what we had in mind."[35] Still, it wasn't until their adult safari decamped to the strip clubs in the shadow of the Strip that the filmmakers found what they were looking for: "the working mothers, derailed students, dumped weekend call girls, and runaway teenagers who would serve as a model [sic] for *Showgirls.*"[36]

The Stardust and the Cheetah are basically mirrors of their star attractions: the former glitters like Cristal while the latter takes its reckless, desperate-to-please vibe from Nomi (who dances there under the stage name of "Heather"). Equal opportunity sleaze merchants, Verhoeven and Eszterhas give both milieus their fair share of screen time, but the film's sympathies are cast squarely with the stragglers on the second tier. Where the Stardust's higher-paid performers screech and claw at each other, the Cheetah's down-and-out dancers seem like one big happy family. In between numbers, the girls all flock to the side of Henrietta "Mama" Bazoom (Lin Tucci), an outsized and outstandingly vulgar woman who functions as a sort of den mother as well as a wisecracking mistress of ceremonies. The father figure is Al (Robert Davi), who commands considerably less affection but no small amount of respect. Just as Nomi had been a stranger backstage at the Stardust, Verhoeven and Eszterhas introduce a newcomer into this cozy showbiz family: Hope, née Penny (Rena Riffel), a slim, busty blonde recruit about to begin her first night on the job.

Once again, the film is playing name games. "My name isn't Hope," the young blonde says cheerfully. "They want class, dum-dum," replies Al in a pained, father-knows-best tone. "They don't want to fuck a Penny. They want to fuck a Heather, or a Tiffany, or a Hope." There's a double entendre here: not only is Eszterhas implying, via his sneering mouthpiece Al, that the Cheetah is a place filled with false Hope(s), he's also using the name Penny to suggest that the girls who come there are just cheap assets waiting to be put into circulation. "If you want to last longer than a week, you'll give me a blowjob," Al taunts the rookie before slinking off to the front. Penny's bewildered expression says it all, but she asks Nomi anyway: "Is he being serious?"

We might ask the same question of the movie. *Showgirls* offers up two answers at the same time. "You know what they call that useless piece of skin around a twat?" inquires Henrietta of the club's sweaty, lecherous audience. Her answer — "A woman!" — wins a spirited round of applause from the punters, who are drooling in anticipation of the next act. Is this a caustic commentary on the cruelty of this milieu, or a screenwriter applauding his own mean-spirited showmanship?

It may be yet another two-for-one proposition, a knowing wink beneath a furrowed brow. The film's attitude towards the Cheetah's howling clientele is unmistakably contemptuous, yet it's doing just as much to prime the audience in the theater for the main event as Henrietta is to whip her customers into a frenzy. And not a moment too soon, because *Showgirls* is finally about to show girls.

It's also about to truly begin to validate its NC-17 rating, which was a hot topic of conversation and speculation in the weeks leading up to its release. In an interview with the *New York Times* two months before *Showgirls*' premiere, Frank Mancuso, then the chairman of MGM/UA, said that he hoped that the "stigma attached to the NC-17 rating [would] be removed" by the fact that the movie was opening on 1,000 screens.[37] Although the NC-17 had been instituted by the Motion Picture Association in 1990 as a slightly-less-restrictive alternative to the dreaded "X" rating, it was still reserved for foreign-language and independent productions. "For several years, film studios have flirted madly with the NC-17, only to back off at the last minute and make the cuts needed to earn an R," wrote William Grimes in another *New York Times* piece. "Just one NC-17 hit would turn attraction into love."[38]

Basic Instinct had been one of those movies snipped in order to avoid inciting the censors' wrath (as had *RoboCop* before it), but this time, Verhoeven refused to budge. "I'm not a crusader," he told the *Times*. "I'm too amoral to care. And it's not to shock. I just don't want to shock myself by cutting my film."[39] By agreeing to defer 70 percent of his salary, Verhoeven was able to retain total creative control over the film and a commitment that MGM/UA would distribute it regardless of its ultimate rating. Which is not to say that certain people involved with the production weren't hoping for a different outcome with the ratings board. "There is nothing to say that this movie will be an NC-17," offered co-producer Frank Marshall. "It doesn't contain a lot of violence, and it doesn't contain a great deal of sex. What it does contain is a great deal of naked bodies."[40]

The most prominent of these, of course, is the one belonging to Elizabeth Berkley, which has until now remained hidden under leather or tightly sheathed in Spandex. Nomi, or "Heather," has two solo stripteases in the first scene at the Cheetah: a Prince-scored pole-dancing number on the club's main stage, and a private performance in the back parlor for Cristal and Zack, who have showed up at the club giggling, coked-out, and looking for a little bit of fun. Cristal is also looking for something more: she's trying to prove her earlier assertion that whatever Nomi does at the Cheetah, it isn't dancing. And Nomi is terrified when she spots the older woman in the audience, only reluctantly allowing herself to be led into the private area after Al insists that the pair's offer of $500 is enough to offset the club rules pertaining to couples and to female patrons.

The Cheetah's other major rule is "Touch and Go," as in "they touch, they go" — an insurance policy against some of the grabbier guests. Whatever her reservations, Nomi sucks it up and gives Cristal and Zack (and the viewer) a heck of a show, undulating all over the latter until he climaxes inside his pants. "What is shocking in the scene is not its frank sexuality, which one could find in plenty of small-budget pornos all over cable or on VHS," writes *Cahiers du cinéma* correspondent Bill Krohn, "but the pedantry of its mise en scène, which uses the venerable grammar of classical cinema to make sure that the dumbest spectator would understand it."[41]

Krohn believes that he is too smart for this scene, and that Verhoeven's ideas about sex and power are "rancid." Both things may be true, but the scene is not without a certain sophistication. Cristal and Zack have enough money and status that they can basically make Nomi do whatever they want, and for whatever reason. In Zack's case, it's for physical gratification, while for Cristal it's the ability to wield power over a woman she sees as a rival and a threat — and also as an object of desire. Though both of her exploiters are making a show of the fact that they're slumming, despite her embarrassment Nomi is able to reduce both of them to jelly through the sheer sensual force of her performance. It's as if her body has briefly become weaponized.

Despite their glib posturing at the start, there is nothing ironic or superior about Cristal and Zack's enjoyment of their private dance. And yet as Cristal counts out the bills in the aftermath, her smug smile returns. For her, $500 is petty cash, and money well spent; for Nomi, it's a windfall. If *Showgirls* is indeed a mirror, then Cristal and Zack are reflections here of the movie's audience, who have also presumably spent good money to see Elizabeth Berkley do her thing in the nude and have, at long last, gotten what they paid for.

This equivalency is even more suggestive when we consider that Zack and Cristal receive their voyeuristic jollies in a back room as opposed to the Cheetah's main stage. Krohn is right to invoke the advent of VHS, because *Showgirls* is a movie with a tortured relationship to home-entertainment systems. In an article for *Cinema Journal* entitled "The Naked Truth: *Showgirls* and the Fate of the X/NC-17 Rating," Kevin Sandler outlines the specifics of *Showgirls'* elaborate marketing campaign, including MGM/UA's pioneering use of separate "green-band" and "red-band" trailers attached to movies with differing MPAA ratings, and the release of an eight-minute home video preview 11 days before the film's premiere: "Free of charge to consumers 18 or over, the video could be picked up at all major retail outlets, except Blockbuster Video."[42]

The demand for these screeners was so great that stores had to order additional copies, and yet when the full movie was released in theaters, the grosses were dismal. Most of the "adult" Hollywood movies greenlit around the same time as (or after) *Showgirls* also did poorly, including William Friedkin's Eszterhas-scripted *Jade* (1995), Andrew Bergman's *Striptease* (1996), and Adrian Lyne's remake of *Lolita* (1997). Even *Eyes Wide Shut*, from the director who was brave enough to try to make *Lolita* in the first place 35 years earlier, flopped, despite being hyped as Kubrick's final film and boasting two A-list (and then-married) Hollywood stars — Tom Cruise and Nicole Kidman — allegedly participating in some risqué business. Less than a decade after *Basic Instinct* had proved that the "erotic thriller" had (uncrossed) legs at the box office, the genre was buckling at the knees.

Sandler speculates that the commercial failure of *Showgirls* had less to do with its NC-17 rating than other industrial factors. "First, the flood of sex thrillers that followed *Basic Instinct* all but drowned the genre's commercial value at the theaters. Second, soft-core eroticism, of the kind that *Showgirls* used as a publicity stunt, could be seen on pay cable and rented at any video store — privately and at a much cheaper price."[43] Sandler also points out that while people seemed hesitant to see *Showgirls* in theaters, "they seemed happy to pay $3 to rent [it] on video"[44] — the spectatorial equivalent of requesting a private dance.

Nomi should be triumphant after scoring her minor victory, but instead she's aggrieved. "You just got $500 for a lap dance, but you're acting like somebody just died," scoffs Al incredulously. She's mad because she's proved Cristal correct. What Nomi does at the Cheetah isn't dancing, exactly. It's closer to what James had said — and what he tells her again the next day when he shows up uninvited at her trailer. "You fuck them without fucking them," he says in his best accusatory tone. "It ain't right. You've got too much talent for it to be right."

James's reward for his backhanded compliment is a door slammed in his face, but when we next see Nomi, she seems to be pondering his observation. Verhoeven films her sitting splay-legged on a park bench in the shadow of a scale model of the Sphinx — two inscrutable women of mystery side by side. Rather than try to solve the riddle of what she's really doing in Las Vegas, however, Nomi opts for the path of least resistance. Under the pretense of celebrating Molly's success on her sewing-school exam, the pair go shopping, an excursion that culminates in Nomi spotting a black-and-gold Versace dress in a shop window and deciding to buy it. "I can make that dress," says Molly, preaching the gospel of simpler pleasures, but Nomi wants to buy it anyway.

The Versace dress is a harbinger of upward mobility. No sooner has Nomi bought it than she's approached at the Cheetah by a talent scout from the Stardust, who tells her that a spot has opened up for a background dancer in "Goddess." The difference between Molly's simple handmade wares and the Versace dress is also the difference between the Cheetah and the Stardust: a designer label disguising a similar manufacture. Nomi's delighted expression when she tells Molly that she got an audition is a rare moment of uncomplicated joy for the character, but it also recalls her ecstatic reaction at the slot machines: a brief flash of pride before the fall. Striding into the Stardust's theater for a group casting call, Nomi looks confident and composed, until *Goddess*'s producer Tony Moss (Alan Rachins) throws her with his greeting: "Hey, Pollyanna . . . I said: you look like Pollyanna."

There are two things that we can say about this. 1) Despite his better suit and lack of visible pockmarks, Tony is cut from the same cloth as Al, right down to the fact that he likes to come up with nicknames for his showgirls; and 2) he recognizes at a glance that Nomi is hopelessly naïve. (He's also right that she looks like a "Pollyanna," as we will see later on.) Momentarily unnerved, Nomi sucks it up and rushes to the mirror at the side of the stage, applies a little blush, removes her top to reveal a purple bra, and gets in line to meet the new boss. Just as Mama's stage patter at the Cheetah sounded like Joe Eszterhas talking out of both sides of his mouth(piece) at the same time — offering up hideously sexist punch lines while making us suspect that the joke was really on those of us who laughed at them — Tony's interrogation of the dancers plays out in a sharply double-edged way; it's almost a misogynist variation on Gunnery Sergeant Hartman's (R. Lee Ermey) profanely homophobic grilling of the Parris Island recruits in Kubrick's *Full Metal Jacket* (1987).

Like Kubrick, Verhoeven tracks the Steadicam up and down the line as Tony surveys the young women vying for a spot in the production. The camera pauses as he insults them, each in turn, with breathtaking callousness. One voluptuous blonde is dismissed because her breasts are too ample ("this isn't a watermelon patch"); another hopeful is mockingly asked if she can "spell MGM backwards" (she can, to no avail). Recognizing one brunette as a previous applicant, he admiringly notes that she's had work done on her nose but that her ears stick out: "Come back and see me when you get them fixed." It's not just physical attributes that Tony is denigrating, however. A raven-haired girl tells Tony that she's had "ice-skating classes, ballet classes, technique classes, stretch classes, jazz classes, jazz technique classes." "The show is called *Goddess*, it ain't called classes," he retorts, echoing Al's earlier comment that the Cheetah was, at the very least, a "class joint."

8

"Show Me Your Tits"

Tony's inspection of the merchandise enters its second phase once he's narrowed the field down to three finalists — including Nomi, who is the only one of the group with the guts (or maybe the naïveté) to throw the insults back in his face. "Show me your tits," Tony exhorts the lucky trio. They look apprehensive, but they don't have a choice; *Goddess* is a topless show, after all. Nomi is not suitably excited by the request. "I'm erect," sneers Tony. "Why aren't you erect?" He proffers a bowl of ice cubes to help Nomi's nipples achieve the requisite rigidity, a gesture that is both literally and figuratively frigid. Nomi throws the cubes in his face and rushes into the wings.

"When Tony . . . auditions a line of hopefuls, picks three and says, 'Show me your tits,' . . . he is acting on behalf of the entire film," writes Anthony Lane.[45] But Linda Williams finesses this point by arguing that all Verhoeven and Eszterhas are doing in this scene is "updating" the venerable cinematic archetype of "the showgirl," "a figure American culture has both celebrated and despised as the quintessential commodification of womanhood," for a "post-Code, post-feminist, and post-Stonewall era in which it is permissible to foreground (and of course to exploit) the new forms of vulgar sexual display made possible by such cultural innovations as the lap dance."[46]

Williams's point is that *Showgirls*' flaunting of its wares is in keeping with the particular cinematic traditions that the filmmakers are attempting to drag, scissor-kicking and screaming, into the 21st century. In this, *Showgirls* is kin to *Basic Instinct*, except that it's not made under the sign of Alfred Hitchcock: it is instead a very deliberate and detailed homage to classic American movie musicals. In Lloyd Bacon's *42nd Street* (1933), a cash-strapped theater director (Warner Baxter) urges a line of auditioning chorines to hike up their skirts so that he can take a gander at their gams — proof positive that *Showgirls*' explicitness is merely a hyperbolized extension of the sexuality inherent in its far-from-innocent musical models.

Of course, the tenor of the times — and the dictates of the soon-to-be instituted Production Code — meant that *42nd Street* was obliged to cleverly channel its sexual content into a series of elaborate, lascivious (though ultimately chaste) production numbers, which were created by the legendary Busby Berkeley. The California-born choreographer was one of the biggest influences on the development of the American film musical, and one of the few artists whose name is used as a descriptive adjective. "The chief structuring elements of the Berkeley aesthetic are so identifiable that he has earned a place in the slang lexicon," writes Pamela Robertson. "'Busby Berkeley: a very elaborate musical number; any bevy of beautiful girls; a spectacular.' The typical Berkeley number showcases scores of beautiful white women who form intricate, fairly abstract patterns, who do not necessarily dance but walk and smile . . . it kaleidoscopes female forms in ever-changing designs."[47] Judith Mayne asserts that Busby Berkeley's "spectaculars lay bare the very mechanisms which in other films would remain concealed," implying that by reducing his female performers to little more than smiling props, the choreographer was disguising sex in geometry, shoving the directly erotic out of view and onto a subliminal plane.

What Verhoeven and Eszterhas do in *Showgirls*, in accordance with the increased permissiveness of their particular historical moment, is collapse the space between Busby Berkeley and Elizabeth Berkley: taking advantage of the license granted them by the unqualified success of *Basic Instinct*, they take the sublimated sex of the Hollywood production number and make it gloriously, vulgarly explicit. But even as they err on the side of excess in comparison to Berkeley's (relatively) tasteful treatment of his interchangeable chorines, Verhoeven and Eszterhas also echo, and build upon, the Depression-era musical's attention to the backstage travails of the hard-working glamour girls, balancing their desire to "show girls" with a determination to show what those girls go through before, during, and after their initiation into their particular showbiz sorority.

Nomi isn't quite there yet, however. Licking her wounds backstage, she looks every inch the Pollyanna that Tony pegged her as, used and bruised by her illusions. No sooner does Nomi leave the Stardust then she is approached by James, now wearing a white bellhop's uniform and trundling luggage through the hotel's entranceway. He doesn't wear the uniform for long, however: after trying to cheer Nomi up and repeating his spiel about how she has more talent than she, or the exploiters selling "tits and ass" at the Stardust, know what to do with, he gets himself fired by telling off his supervisor and tossing the jacket in the man's startled face, much like Nomi dumped the ice all over Tony's shirt.

James resolves to take Nomi out for some fun, which first involves buying her some fast food (a greasy cheeseburger that she devours with her customary gusto) and asking her where she's from. Note that Nomi's response — "different places" — is the same one that she gave Molly on their fast-food date. If we already know that Molly and Nomi are on the same continuum of kindness (at least toward each other), it seems, for the time being, that James is there too. For all his harsh assessments of Nomi's dancing and his accusations about her "teasing his dick," he's someone who she can trust.

Nomi and James arrive at the latter's rundown flat on a similar footing, having both angrily rejected gigs at the Stardust. They're also both horny, and quickly dispense with small talk in favor of rehearsing the modern-dance revue that James hopes to mount at the Crave Club. At first, Nomi diligently mirrors the steps that James is showing her, but she quickly lapses into the same slinky maneuvers she'd demonstrated in the back room at the Cheetah. Not that James seems to mind. Like Tony, he gestures to see Nomi's breasts and she obliges him, adding a deep kiss as she writhes in his lap. But when he goes for her crotch, she stops him by purring that she has her period (which had also been her excuse to Al about missing work the night she'd been arrested for inciting a riot). Just as with Cristal and Zack, Nomi is fucking James without actually fucking him, simultaneously proving the truth of the latter's accusations while exposing his motivations as having less to do with collaboration than copulation.

James's conflicted responses derive from Nomi's mixed signals, as Linda Williams observes: "The line between fucking and dancing is blurred at every turn . . . whenever Nomi dances, she seems to be having sex, and whenever she has sex, she seems to be dancing; there is no pure sexual desire and there is no pure dance anywhere in *Showgirls*."[48] In light of later revelations about her character, Nomi's physical embodiment of this slippage makes perfect sense, while James's attempts to neatly compartmentalize between aesthetic and biological imperatives will be in vain. As Nomi leaves with her virtue intact, he accuses her of being confused about who she is — but what he's really describing are his own reasons for bringing her home in the first place.

This disorientation is confirmed a few short scenes later, after Nomi has gotten the call from Tony Moss to report to the Stardust for the role in *Goddess*. Elated by this change of scenery, she marches into the Cheetah — her strides aligned with a green neon arrow mounted in the hallway — to get her things. After blowing off Henrietta and Al, who mock her aspirations and suggest that she'll come crawling back to the Cheetah in short order, Nomi rushes back to James's place to give him the good news. His self-righteous irritation that she's chosen the bright lights of the Strip over their artistic endeavor is undermined by the fact that he's currently sleeping with Penny, who, having already been positioned by the film-makers as Nomi's double, has gladly charged up the path her doppelgänger chose to leave untaken.

The scene pivots on shameless dramatic cliché: the sudden and unexpected discovery by the heroine of another woman in her beloved's bed, a staple of romantic comedies and afternoon soap operas as ritualized and predictable as the scare chords in a horror movie. Yet the scene is also complicated in the way it bounces three separate characters' delusions off one another. Penny believes that sleeping with James will be her shortcut to stardom, but she's no less interchangeable to him than she was to Al at the Cheetah; this time, she's conjuring up her own false Hope, and clinging to it for dear life. James slips once again into the role of the rejected mentor, pleading clemency in the name of artistic integrity, but as soon as Nomi is gone, he tells Penny that she's a great dancer and that he wrote the piece for her. And while Nomi sees right through James and his urban-sage act, she's blind to the fact that she's following that big green glowing arrow straight into the belly of the beast.

When she shows up for work at the Stardust, Nomi has opted for her beloved Versace dress. "When you first walked in here, you looked like Pollyanna . . . now you look like, I don't know, Lolita," growls Tony Moss. It's a lousy line, but one of the funniest and most quotable moments in *Showgirls* comes immediately thereafter when Nomi responds to a compliment about her outfit by saying, "Thanks, it's Ver-sayce." This sincere mispronunciation of the designer's name italicizes her blue-collar upbringing. The *Goddess* creative team laughs off the blunder, but they don't go easy on Nomi. After being subjected to some HR questions about her past (which she bravely bluffs her way through), she's read the riot act by Dee about everything from her diet ("You do like brown rice and vegetables, don't you?") to her recreational activities ("Stay inside. No tan lines."), and then put through her paces in an intense rehearsal that requires her to learn several numbers' worth of hard-thrusting choreography seemingly in minutes. Finally, she's thrown onstage as a topless background dancer in the evening performance, which goes well except for the part where the first-timer accidentally steps in some "monkey shit" left behind by a chimpanzee who'd broken loose of his Siegfried and/or Roy–looking trainer.

The speed with which Nomi goes from bumbling misfit to hardy trouper is blatantly and artificially accelerated. *Showgirls* is powering through each stage of its heroine's ascent in order to bring her closer to her dream, and also to her rival. At this point in the movie, the characters who have been employed as friends and foils to Nomi start to fall away. Another parking-lot encounter with James merely rehashes his betrayal and restates his claims that he can spur Nomi on to greater artistic achievement than her new bosses, whom he characterizes as "pimps." And even though Nomi rather conspicuously tells Molly that she loves her before running onstage, she really only has (narrow, suspicious, desirous) eyes for her co-star Cristal. At every step of Nomi's ascent, Cristal has been there in the background as a mass-produced poster image in the Stardust's driveway.

Showgirls is a movie very clearly bisected into two parts. There is a fade to black after Nomi and Molly laughingly drive away from James, and then the lights come up again on the Stardust's stage as Nomi enters frame left. It's a reverse-mirror image of the film's first scene, right down to the fact that Nomi is wearing her leather jacket. Cristal greets her in full cowgirl drag, snorting coke out of a snuffbox and offering to help Nomi work on her steps — a transparently phony offer that contains a ring of truth. "I'm feeling turned inside out today," offers Cristal, and well she should. As the rest of this sequence plays out, she might as well be having an out-of-body experience.

Just as Nomi had (perhaps unconsciously) copied Cristal while watching her run through *Goddess* during her first visit to the Stardust, she begins to sync their movements together from the other side of their table at Spago. While chatting, Nomi extends her hand, which is clenched around a corn chip, until it brushes against Cristal's fingers. This tortilla toast presages an actual one with champagne, which Nomi says gives her a headache but Cristal deems holy water, prompting a flirty, fizzy, finger-flicked baptismal that Nomi returns a few seconds later. "You and me, we're exactly alike," purrs the older woman, as if the choreography of the scene hadn't made that (Cristal) clear already.

This scene poses a particularly challenging Masterpiece/ Piece of Shit conundrum. Many critics singled out Nomi and Cristal's exchanges in this scene as the most damning evidence of Eszterhas's maladroit way with dialogue. Not only is there discussion of a shared fondness for eating dog food, but there's also Cristal's assessment of her own silicone-enhanced transformation from farm girl to Goddess ("It's amazing what paint and a surgeon can do"), her compliment to Nomi ("You have great tits, they're really beautiful"), and Nomi's breathy retort ("I like having nice tits"). And so it goes, until they're interrupted by a party of Texan autograph seekers whom Cristal finesses with a little homespun charm. Rick Groen of the *Globe and Mail* wrote that Eszterhas's tactic of "putting his most misogynistic remarks in the mouths of women" was "a ruse that even Camille Paglia should see through,"[49] while in the *New York Times*, Janet Maslin referred to the "soul-numbing stupidity" of the screenwriting, which she believed prevented "any character from entertaining two consecutive thoughts in a given scene."[50]

But why settle for two consecutive thoughts when you can be of two minds at the same time? The writing in this scene may be blunt, but the filmmaking is supple, starting with the fact that Verhoeven violates the 180-degree rule — the unwritten law that in any dialogue sequence, the axis joining the characters will remain consistent — about midway through the scene. For the first half of the scene, Cristal is on the left side of the table and Nomi on the right, with Verhoeven cutting between them in turn as they speak. After the champagne comes out, however, the positions are reversed: Nomi is in Cristal's place, and vice versa. The subliminal visual effect is of two women talking to themselves, which undercuts Nomi's protest to Cristal that "I'll never be like you." The contrast between the overstatement of the dialogue and the subtlety of the direction mirrors the contrast in the performance styles of Berkley and Gershon, which is more evident than ever — and which is the exact same dynamic that's supposed to be playing out between the two characters. Good filmmaking propping up bad screenwriting; a bad actress dragging down a good one. It's all in plain view.

9

"If Somebody Gets in Your Way, Step on 'Em"

Returning to the still-deserted stage area, Cristal dispenses some more hard-earned wisdom — "If somebody gets in your way, step on 'em" — before making good on her promise and leading Nomi through her paces. (The question of how Nomi knows the choreography for the ensuing pas de deux is left unanswered. Perhaps she's such a dance prodigy that she can immediately pick up a routine that she's apparently never rehearsed before.) Like James and Tony Moss before her (and Zack soon afterward), Cristal is hell-bent on getting her hands on Nomi's breasts, caressing her from behind, then violently yanking her top off and circling her aureoles before delivering *le mot juste*: "You see darling, you are a whore." As is her wont, Nomi flees the scene, repulsed once again by the suggestion that she's anything less than pure in her aspirations, though perhaps having also taken some mental notes about what to do the next time that Cristal digs in her stiletto heels and impedes her own forward progress.

Both of these lessons — the one about being a whore and the one about doing anything to get ahead — will play out over the next few scenes. Invited to dance at a convention for $1,000 (a gig arranged at Cristal's behest), Nomi discovers that she's really supposed to entertain (read: sleep with) the hotel's high-rolling guest from Bangkok (would Eszterhas have had him hail from any other city?), and, for those of us keeping count, makes her fifth furious exit of the film. Nomi confronts Zack on the *Goddess* stage and demands an apology, but Zack's subsequent dressing-down of the employee who booked the gig is just for show: as soon as Nomi is out of earshot, Zack calls him back (on his toaster-sized mobile phone) to chortle about their charade. His concern for Nomi's virtue is as ersatz as the papier-mâché volcanoes behind him.

The push-or-be-pushed mentality, meanwhile, plays out when Nomi spots her cast-mate Julie (Melissa Williams) laying a trap for the thoroughly obnoxious Annie (Ungela Brockman), with whom she has been feuding for the entire run of the show. Dressed to the nines for a very Busby Berkeley–ish ballroom-themed number, Julie scatters some phony diamonds on the stage, causing Annie's partner to trip and send Annie crashing to the ground. Verhoeven cuts between the dancer in agony on the floor and Cristal ascending via hidden wires towards the ceiling. While they're on separate trajectories, this is a hint that in Cristal's case, what goes up will also come down.

It is here that Eszterhas and Verhoeven's references to *42nd Street* become obvious. In that film, an untested ingénue (Ruby Keeler) gets a chance to be a Broadway star after the show's leading lady fractures her ankle, and after the official understudy (Ginger Rogers) concedes that she's not ready for her moment in the spotlight; similarly, Annie's injury paves the way for Nomi to take over as Cristal's understudy. But where the chorines in *42nd Street* stick up for each other unequivocally, in *Showgirls* their sisterly solidarity is more selective and self-serving: Nomi doesn't rat out Julie, and her reward for playing dumb is a chance at a promotion.

This is workplace advancement as survival of the fittest; one is reminded of the satire of chain-of-command politics in Verhoeven's subsequent *Starship Troopers*, where fresh-faced yokel Johnny Rico (Casper Van Dien) keeps going up in rank as his peers and superior officers are mowed down in battle. Released in November 1997, *Starship Troopers* was something of a comeback for Verhoeven after the dismal box-office reception of *Showgirls*, doing respectable if not massive business and prompting comments that the director was better off sticking with violent science fiction instead of erotic spectacle. And yet, despite their obvious differences in scale and subject matter, *Starship Troopers* and *Showgirls* are actually very similar in their approach: they simultaneously fully inhabit and mercilessly satirize their respective genres, duly delivering the goods while playing up their toxicity. In a review for *Entertainment Weekly*, Owen Gleiberman wrote, "With *Starship Troopers*, [Verhoeven] is trashing movies even as he makes a brazenly entertaining one."[51]

While *Starship Troopers* is packed with brutally violent and astonishingly well-realized special effects sequences that suggest *Saving Private Ryan* (1998) by way of *Star Wars* (1977), it also gives us several cues that we risk getting swept up in this spectacle at our own peril. In adapting Robert A. Heinlein's famously militaristic 1959 novel, Verhoeven and his screenwriter Edward Neumeier (who also penned *RoboCop*) transformed the story from a gung-ho endorsement of a fully mobilized society to a skeptical parody of media propaganda. Not only do the interstitial segments emanating from the ugly American "Federal News Network" spoof the style of World War II newsreels (*Why We Fight* with laser guns instead of bayonets), the stentorian narrator's repeated query — "Would you like to know more?" — is bluntly ironic, given the clear evidence that these "news items" are little more than state-sanctioned disinformation.

Although *Starship Troopers* had its detractors, the general consensus was that Verhoeven and Neumeier were doing something subversive, which was all the more impressive for going largely undetected by the mass audience that had shown up to see sleekly armored pretty-boy soldiers mow down scores of CGI arachnids. But when reviewers rightly connected these qualities in *Starship Troopers* to similar tactics in *RoboCop* (which also mocked credulous mass-market journalism), they made a point of skipping over *Showgirls*, as if it represented a break in the continuity of its maker's career. Chon Noriega singles out Anthony Lane's assertion that "there is not a whisper of satire in [*Showgirls*]" as an example of how critics missed out on the film's distinctively Verhoevian jokes.[52]

When Henrietta and Al surprise Nomi backstage in the aftermath of Annie's accident — greeting her like loving country-bumpkin parents who've journeyed from the farm to the big city to see their girl strut her stuff on the stage, Nomi smiles fondly at the man who had previously made a habit of hitting her up for blowjobs and the soundtrack suddenly melts into corn syrup — it's as if the movie is trying and failing to keep a straight face. The mask cracks once and for all with Al's weirdly wistful parting shot after their tender reunion: "It must be weird not to have people coming on you."

Rather than taking Al's 180-degree turn from lecherous pimp-manqué to lovable daddy-dearest at face value — i.e., as evidence of lazy direction and/or terrible screenwriting — it seems more likely that the humor is wholly intentional. (Who needs a "whisper of satire" when you can have a big old belly laugh?) Considering what we know of Al, his seal of approval wouldn't seem to be worth the wax it's stamped on. And yet it's also apparent that Al and Henrietta's honest, unrepentant vulgarity is somehow nobler in Eszterhas's eyes than the slick, cynical exploitation of a man like Zack, who suggestively slithers onscreen seconds after Al departs and whisks Nomi away to his swanky bachelor pad.

The casting here is witty, since MacLachlan was best

known at this point in his career for playing wide-eyed straight-arrows who get perversely bent out of shape in David Lynch's *Blue Velvet* (1986) and the Lynch/Mark Frost cult TV series *Twin Peaks* (1990–1991). Here, he's a smooth operator, a prototypical yuppie scumbag: where James had to ply Nomi with promises of artistic fulfillment, Zack simply shows off his car and his modern art collection then sits back and watches while his guest undresses herself, no seduction required. She then slips naked into the swimming pool, where Zack douses her in champagne — Cristal, of course — and then basically just stands there while she proceeds to ravish him as water beats down on them from a dolphin-shaped fountain.

In 2005, the British entertainment magazine *Empire* voted Nomi and Zack's soggy coupling as "the crappiest movie sex sequence of all time." "It's supposed to be the best sex in the world," carps the article's author, "but, as Berkley thrashes around in the water, it looks more like the first ten minutes of *Jaws*."[53] What it actually looks like, however, is Nomi and Zack's previous encounter at the Cheetah, with Nomi once again doing all the work: Zack barely moves at all during the scene, while Nomi thrashes her ambitious little heart out. A close-up of water splattering over her face and breasts as she flops around moaning in apparent ecstasy is framed like a porn-film money shot — which in a way it is, since this is the only consensual sex scene in this NC-17 movie.

The pool scene is absurd, yes. Full stop. It is also, despite its show-stopping qualities, very much of a piece with the rest of the movie, both in terms of Berkley's acting (which is game, guileless, and over the top, as always), and also in what it reveals about Nomi: namely, that she has been wholly consumed by her star-gazing ambitions. "You can fuck me when you love me," she'd told James, and yet because Zack can seemingly offer so much more than the lowly choreographer, he's able to swiftly bypass this edict. When Molly sees Nomi the next day, she cautions her friend ("Don't get sucked into it"), but it's too late. Zack bullies Tony into making Nomi Cristal's understudy, a decision that does not sit well with the territorial top-liner. "You shouldn't get pissed off, it makes you look older," grins Nomi, finally enjoying the pleasures of having the upper hand.

It doesn't last long, however. After a brief trip to the Crave Club to catch up with James, Nomi returns to the Stardust to find that Zack has rescinded his offer. Cristal has put her foot down, and as she holds court in front of Nomi's dressing-room mirror, with the sheet of paper bearing Nomi's name suggestively tacked above her head, she sarcastically inquires about whether she can get her nails done some time. The claws are coming out.

Just as Nomi and Cristal's lunch date was quickly followed by a dance sequence physicalizing the pair's sexual and professional power struggle, this latest confrontation gets replayed onstage for all to see. In *Showgirls: Portrait of a Film*, Verhoeven credits his choreographer, Marguerite Pomerhn-Derricks, with coming up with the idea for "The Avenging Angel," an S&M-themed production number that finds the members of the *Goddess* troupe done up in leather fetish gear in a smoky warehouse setting.[54] Nomi even rides a motorcycle onstage, only to be topped by Cristal, who is introduced dangling precariously from a rope. Menaced by the male gang members in a fashion that suggests a Kenneth Anger production of *West Side Story* (1961), she fights them off and settles into a duet with Nomi that's simultaneously hostile and erotic. They aren't dancing with each other so much as *at* each other, and Cristal even trips Nomi in the middle of a maneuver, which she's able to do without breaking character since she's playing the queen of the writhing biker chicks. "Let's go, slave girl," she taunts, leading her partner (by the throat) off the stage and to the top of the stairs — at which point an hour-and-a-half's worth of foreshadowing finally pays off, and Nomi pushes her all the way down.

The bigger they are, the harder they fall. Cristal has to this point been one of the most powerful characters in the film, certainly the one who holds the most sway over Nomi. Her incapacitation post–stair-pushing has a momentous narrative fallout: the Stardust's power brokers have no choice but to insert Nomi — who feigns innocence over the incident, and is backed up by Julie in a gesture of reciprocal sneakiness — into the lead role of *Goddess*. "We'll do what we always do in Las Vegas," proclaims Zack heroically. "We'll gamble."

The gamble pays off, as Nomi fills Cristal's shoes admirably — but it also throws the entire dramaturgy of the movie out of whack. To this point, *Showgirls* has patiently, even methodically, run through the conventions of its rising-star narrative, emphasizing not only Nomi's talent and ambition in pursuit of her goals, but also the many obstacles in her way. Cristal's move to the sidelines means that there's nothing holding Nomi down anymore. If *Showgirls* is a modern gloss on *All About Eve*, it's as if Bette Davis had been rudely dispatched two-thirds of the way through, leaving us with Anne Baxter.

For a little while, it seems like Nomi won't have her faithful sidekick to help her along the way. Nomi's obsessive fixation on Cristal had more or less pushed Molly out of the story, but after the accident she reappears, fixing her roommate with a stricken, judgmental expression. She doesn't come right out and accuse Nomi of pushing Cristal, but she's suspicious. It's quietly jarring when Nomi, now moved into Cristal's dressing room, ignores Molly picking up after her like a personal assistant. Nomi only has eyes for Zack, who comes bearing gifts and promises of a chic after party. When Molly finally confronts Nomi about Cristal's accident, the answer is a denial and a flat-out lie — and both women know it. The sense of luckless solidarity that linked Molly to Nomi in those early scenes — her identification with and attraction to a woman who had been treated badly by life — is replaced by disappointment and disgust, and also maybe some guilt about her own complicity in what's gone down; after all, it was Molly who invited Nomi to the Stardust in the first place.

In another reversal, it is Nomi who now invites Molly to go behind the scenes, to a private party hosted by Zack and featuring an appearance by Andrew Carver (William Shockley), the lion-tressed rock star who is Molly's biggest celebrity crush. It's hard to tell exactly which early '90s pop beefcake this character is supposed to be spoofing (Michael Bolton?), but it doesn't really matter, because Andrew Carver is arguably the one person in *Showgirls* who it is impossible to laugh with, or at. Where the other repugnant men on hand either filter their cruelty through polished power-gaming (Zack) or are revealed as toothless tigers (Tony Moss and Al), Andrew Carver has no layers to shed, no secret rottenness to reveal. From the moment he meets Nomi at the party and tells her under his breath that he likes her ass, he's an uncomplicatedly loathsome lothario.

And yet Molly, who sees Nomi for what she has become, is still mesmerized by him, and shows up at the party — done up in the sort of fancy dress she'd told Nomi wasn't worth the money she'd paid for it — hoping to initiate a seduction. Just as James's claims of artistic integrity were undermined by his libido, Molly allows herself to be led astray by her desires — to be led, in fact, into Andrew Carver's private suite, where she is in short order savagely beaten and raped by her fake white knight and two members of his entourage.

Molly's rape is, without a doubt, the most uncomfortable sequence in *Showgirls*, and one that violently resists any sort of winking, tongue-in-cheek re-appropriation. Where the previous striptease and sex scenes were geared toward titillation, Molly's encounter with Andrew Carver is appropriately brutal and nightmarish, and the relative restraint of the staging — the camera cuts away just as one of Carver's goons climbs on top of the screaming, defenseless, and bleeding woman on the bed — heightens the horror of the proceedings. The filmmaking is undeniably effective, but what's harder to gauge is whether a scene this unsettling belongs in this movie.

10

"We Just Want to Party, Baby"

In an incredibly disturbing scene in *Spetters*, one of the protagonists, Eve (Toon Agterberg) — who we have earlier seen engaging in gay-bashing rhetoric — is gang-raped in a subway tunnel by a gang of leather-clad thugs, which makes him realize that he is himself homosexual and results in him coming out to his strict, Bible-thumping father. "One hates to think what the reaction to this film would have been if it had been a woman, rather than a man, who must thus testify to the therapeutic effects of rape," wrote Vincent Canby in the *New York Times*, implying that Verhoeven was somehow employing and exploiting a sexual double standard.[55] But this is almost a willful misreading of the scene in question. Far from testifying to the "therapeutic effects of rape," *Spetters* shows just how far its bike-riding anti-heroes' self-images as cocksure young hunks are from their dismal real lives on the social and economic margins. *Spetters* is a film about three young men who fancy themselves swashbuckling knights but are really just pawns, expendable riders on the fast track to nowhere.

While the rape scene undoubtedly stands out, *Spetters* is a movie where violence, sexual duplicity, and despair are never too far out of sight. In *Showgirls*, the attack on Molly points to things that are barely concealed. Verhoeven cross-cuts between Molly's ordeal and the rest of the partygoers swaying obliviously to a jazzy rendition of Eurythmics' "Walk into the Wind," with the camera eventually settling on Nomi and Zack in a romantic clinch. If we didn't know that this was a party being thrown in honor of a soft-core Vegas spectacular, the gathering might look like a record-industry shindig or a high-end corporate confab (or even the New Year's ball in Kubrick's *The Shining*). The elegance of the party is arranged in stark, obvious juxtaposition to the ugliness of what is going on behind closed doors, and while this contrast is anything but subtle, it's no less powerful for that. When Molly suddenly staggers out into the middle of the dance floor and collapses in a splayed, bloody heap, it's genuinely shocking.

Kubrick achieved a similar effect in the early scenes of *Eyes Wide Shut*, when the gold-trimmed Christmas soiree thrown by Sydney Pollack's high-society maven is briefly interrupted by the near-fatal overdose of a hooker stashed in one of the upstairs bathrooms. Neat-freak Kubrick frames the girl's peril as decorously as a pietà, while Verhoeven favors a blunter approach, but the implication in both movies is that something is rotting underneath all those alluring surfaces. *Eyes Wide Shut* could also give *Showgirls* a run in the mirrors/doubling department. Not only does Tom Cruise's Bill Harford come face-to-face with his doppelgänger (a hilarious scene featuring *Criminal Mind*'s Thomas Gibson), but the Christmas party scene, with its well-attired revelers turning a blind eye to their host's dirty little secret, gets an operatic B-side with the infamous costume ball/orgy sequence, a lavish redux featuring the same revelers, their inner ugliness now externalized via *commedia dell'arte* masks.

James Naremore has written brilliantly about masks in Kubrick's films, and identified the Janus-faced quality that permits comedy and horror to co-exist within individual scenes (like Sergeant Hartmann's abuse of the troops in *Full Metal Jacket*) and across entire films (the commingling of the unaccountably freaky and the outright farcical in *The Shining*). Naremore characterizes this quality as an "unresolved tension" derived from the literary tradition of the grotesque, which dates back to the picaresque epics of Rabelais and Cervantes. Typically focused on striving, anti-heroic characters navigating a hostile realm, picaresque texts (which are widely understood to be the primary forerunner of the modern novel) are defined more by their gory digressions than their clear narrative progression. In his 1989 study of the history of picaresque fiction, Ulrich Wicks emphasizes the centrality of grotesquerie to the development and popularity of the genre. "The primary function of grotesque motifs in picaresque fiction," Wicks writes, "is to arouse a shocked response from us, to pummel us into an awareness and reaction to the nightmare world of chaos. Grotesque motifs tend to emphasize the unpredictable tendency of the normal to shift suddenly into abnormalcy and horror."[56]

As Naremore identifies Kubrick as updating the tradition of the grotesque, so we can identify Verhoeven as working in the allied tradition of the picaresque. His films tend to favor lone-wolf heroes or heroines finding their way through perilous landscapes; they are frequently episodic in their construction, and their tone often veers toward the satirical. And like many picaresque narratives, they fairly revel in images of bodily excess. Many of Verhoeven's signature sequences are aggressively grotesque: in addition to the trampled henchman in *Total Recall*, there is the eponymous heroine of *Katie Tippel* plunging a co-worker's face into a scalding vat of chemical cleaning solution; the lacerating cutaway in *RoboCop* to a thug whose body has been drenched in acidic, flesh-rending toxins; or the infamous "shower" scene in *Black Book* (2006) where the heroine gets bathed in excrement.

The rape scene in *Showgirls* can thus be understood as an example of capital-G Grotesque: an explosion of the unresolvable tension between unrestrained female eroticism and barely sheathed phallic violence that's been building up for the entire movie. Its aberrance is heightened in proportion to the movie around it, since *Showgirls* is from beginning to end an exercise in bodily excess. Where movies as narratively and dramaturgically distinct as *Katie Tippel* and *Starship Troopers* can be reconciled by their sudden and memorable bursts of carnality (like the unlikely revelation of co-ed military showers in the latter, which interrupts a science-fiction epic for a little bit of *Porky's*-style leering), *Showgirls* features naked breasts and bodies in probably half of its scenes. In terms of Verhoeven's overarching filmmaking strategies, then, the rape scene can be read in two ways at once: as an inversion of his usual M.O., which is to insert sexually explicit scenes into stories that more comfortably support acts of violence, and as a disarming reversal of the typically ecstatic tenor of his sex scenes, from *Turkish Delight's* wild, love-struck copulations to *Basic Instinct's* stylized yet undeniably mutually fulfilling "fuck of the century" between Catherine and Nick.

In terms of its narrative function within the plot of *Showgirls*, however, Molly's rape can really only be understood and looked at in one light: it confirms that this tidy little corner of Las Vegas is truly Sin City, a place where the innocent (Molly) suffer and the wicked (Andrew Carver and his cronies) go officially unpunished. Even Zack doesn't seem wholly convinced by his explanation to Nomi outside Molly's hotel room that Andrew Carver can't be prosecuted because "he may be at the Stardust next season." But he doesn't have to waste too much time rationalizing because he has Nomi dead to rights: he's discovered the secret she wouldn't share with Molly or James, which is that she's really a runaway orphan whose parents died in a murder-suicide, and whose rap sheet includes arrests for drug possession, assault, and soliciting. Eszterhas's fetish for name games comes full circle here, as even the cipher of "Nomi" is revealed to be a phony: the name on Zack's printout reads "Polly Ann Costello." When Tony

Moss had told his new charge, "you look like Pollyanna," he had been on to something.

The revelation of Nomi's troubled background, and Zack's implication that he's going to hold it over her forever while she continues to make a lot of money for the Stardust, is the final turning point in *Showgirls*. Confronted by the very demons she's been trying so desperately to outrun, Nomi suffers intense shame, not least because her strident denials of being a "whore" have now been rendered factually untrue. At the same time, her humiliation also prompts her to let go of the notion that she needs to succeed Cristal as Las Vegas's reigning Goddess. Nomi's fluctuating between doe-eyed naïveté and careerist cynicism has finally come to an end. And while she's as drained as she would be at the end of any shift at the Cheetah Club, she isn't too tired to put on her boogie shoes one more time, for a command performance that might possibly avenge Molly and atone for her past sins in one fell swoop (or, rather, one swift kick).

Before we can get to Nomi's redemption, however, we should briefly consider whether the late-breaking insertion of some backstory does anything to redeem Berkley's performance. For instance, does the knowledge that Nomi used to habitually smoke crack perhaps account for the wild extremity of so many of the actress's gestures, or for her hairpin turns from rage to joy and back again? If this information doesn't retroactively validate the acting itself, could it not at least mean that Berkley gets some points for *trying* to get inside that kind of damaged, frazzled headspace? Or, conversely, if it's possible to discern a satirical perspective in Verhoeven and Eszterhas's contributions to *Showgirls*, then mightn't we wonder if Berkley is actually in on the joke too?

In Mervyn LeRoy's *Gold Diggers of 1933* (1933), a young woman named Polly — once again played by ingénue specialist Ruby Keeler — becomes the leader of a troupe of showgirls who consciously adopt the shameless mannerisms of cash-strapped, mercenary tramps. Because it's the Great Depression, they need to do whatever they can to stay afloat; the opening Busby Berkley–choreographed production number for "We're in the Money," which finds Ginger Rogers singing of her new-found largesse in front of a row of giant golden coins, is point-edly framed as a hopelessly optimistic fantasy, or a bitter satire of such.

In her book *Guilty Pleasures*, Pamela Robertson considers *Gold Diggers of 1933* through the conceptual framework of the "masquerade," a theory previously developed by Mary Ann Doane to describe a stylized form of distaff acting. "The masquerade, in flaunting femininity, holds it at a distance," writes Doane. "Womanliness becomes a mask that can be worn or removed."[57] For Doane, this mask is an embedded address from an actress to the female members of her audience that calls attention to her performance's gendered exaggerations, affirming the distance between performer and character and thus collapsing the female stereotype onscreen.

Taking off from Doane, Robertson argues that the pro-tagonists of *Gold Diggers of 1933* "parody the stereotype of the 'gold digger,' exaggerating [her] traits for comic effect, hyperbolizing the gold digger's masquerade, theatricalizing it to create an ironic distance from it" — and to survive in a world where their opportunities for more gainful or honorable employment are severely limited. This theatricalizing of a hyper-feminine person becomes a form of "feminist camp" that reverses Susan Sontag's contention that camp was especially aligned with a homosexual male sensibility. While acknowledging that Berkeley's production numbers are extravagantly campy in a traditional sense of "style over content," Robertson provocatively suggests that *Gold Diggers of 1933* is also a hotbed of feminist camp. Its superficially bubble-headed showgirl heroines are subsumed into the abstract spectacle of the musical sequences but can also be reclaimed as Depression-era avatars of female ingenuity and endurance, with the actresses continually signifying through their stylized acting that they are as self-aware as their characters.

Showgirls' relationship to camp is a little tougher to suss out. Self-described "missionary of bad taste" Ara Osterweil describes her experience teaching a course in trash cinema at UC Berkeley and having her students react with horror at the inclusion of *Showgirls* on her syllabus. Their primary objection to the movie's inclusion was that it was "unintentionally funny," as opposed to self-consciously cheesy. "By disregarding *Showgirls* because of its perceived lack of ironic intent," writes Osterweil, "my students were dialectally reversing Susan Sontag's dictum that the best or 'purest' kind of camp was naïve rather than deliberate. Although Sontag claims that the 'essential element' in naïve or pure camp is 'a seriousness that fails,' my students had fixated upon Verhoeven's failed seriousness as the very factor that eliminated the film from any valid camp appreciation. Had Verhoeven been trying to create a text saturated in chintzy artifice, histrionic affectation, and absurd sexual display, it would have been the most brilliant piece of camp they'd ever seen. Without this trace of distanciation, *Showgirls* was doomed."[58]

It should hopefully be apparent by this point that it is actually quite easy to perceive the "traces of distanciation" that Osterweil's students seemed to ignore. Recall the impassioned words of Hansen-Løve's Arnaud when his beloved movie is dismissed as trash: "But it's on purpose! Verhoeven directs [Elizabeth Berkley] like that to emphasize his take on things. He accentuates the monstrosity. He's targeting the vulgarity of the United States! This is the third time I've shown it to you and you still don't understand. It's pathetic!" One doesn't have to browbeat one's houseguests to make the point that an auteur previously recognized by critics as a satirist (and a reckless one at that) is unlikely to have shackled those tendencies for a single film before reclaiming them immediately afterward. There's enough evidence in *Showgirls* and the movies before and after it in Verhoeven's filmography to suggest that "failed seriousness" is impossible when the director in question has a chronic problem with dislodging his tongue from his cheek.

The stronger case, perhaps, is that Eszterhas's script is a failure. It is certainly a less shapely piece of work than *Basic Instinct*, which had an irresistible plot hook (Is Catherine Tramell a killer or not?) and several narrative tricks up its sleeve. *Showgirls'* ascendant-ingénue plot has a ritualized quality that belies any real element of surprise (even the revelation of Nomi's "real" identity is predictable, with lots of clues buried in the script). So Eszterhas has to do other things in order to get a rise out of his audience — such as making his dialogue calculatedly outrageous. This is not the same thing as incoherent screenwriting, however. The deeply wrought doubling motifs in the script — the mirroring of certain exchanges, locations, and characters — easily repudiate the accusations of rank incoherence. The screenplay of *Showgirls* may be strident, but it is not naïvely "stupid" in the way that would support a Sontagian sticker of "pure camp" approval.

And so it goes that those inclined to file *Showgirls* under "camp" are left with no choice but to bring things back to Elizabeth Berkley. One might say that Berkley's performance manifests a backward version of the feminist camp process described by Pamela Robertson: instead of a seasoned comic performer using her abilities to signal some distance from her role — becoming a camp producer rather than a camp object — we get the "Jessie Spano Caffeine Pill Freakout" stretched out over two hours. Berkley's performance is not simply "failed seriousness," but "seriously failed seriousness." It's also quite possibly what her director was aiming for.

It would be impossible to prove that Paul Verhoeven deliberately encouraged Berkley to do maladroit work, and it might also be beside the point. The performance is what it is, and both *Showgirls* the Masterpiece and *Showgirls* the Piece of Shit are unimaginable without it. A version of *Showgirls* starring, say, Alicia Silverstone — a credible teen temptress in *The Crush* (1993) and a superior *Saved by the Bell* type in *Clueless* (1995) — might have been a "better" movie owing to the fact that Silverstone was, at the time, a far more capable actress than Berkley. But you probably wouldn't be reading a book about that movie.

If someone did want to make a case for deliberate directorial tampering, Sharon Stone would have been a good witness for the prosecution. She claimed that Verhoeven had kept her in the dark about his true intentions during the shooting of the interrogation scene in *Basic Instinct*, and it would hardly be out of character for him to expose Berkley on a bigger scale, especially if, as in *Basic Instinct*, he believed that it was for the good of the film — and especially if that film was intended as a cautionary tale about inexperienced women becoming grist for the showbiz mill. The lesson of *Showgirls*, according to Verhoeven, is that "at each rung of the ladder, [Nomi] learns she has to pay a higher and higher price for what she is getting."[59] Even before crossing the state line into Nevada, both Nomi and Elizabeth Berkley are headed for a fall, but neither of them knows it yet. With this in mind, the solitary connotations of the character's adopted surname become rather poignant, as they apply equally to the young woman playing her. Nomi (M)Alone, indeed.

11

"Goodbye, Darlin'"

In YouTube clips of Elizabeth Berkley promoting *Showgirls*, she seems as blissfully unaware as Detective Nick Curran of the sword hanging over her head. In an appearance on *Late Show with David Letterman*, she predicts good things for her debut and even offers the host a (very G-rated) lap dance — all in good fun, right? Yet when describing the film, Berkley sounds very much like a nervous kid reciting from a press kit. She also smiles gamely (and in a very practiced way) when recounting how the all-male crew gave her tips about shooting the various striptease sequences.

When *Showgirls* began to get pounded from every conceivable angle after its release, Berkley retreated from view. "I felt like I was the kid on the playground and all of the bullies were being really relentless. It was not a nice time," she said in a 2008 chat on AOL.com. The interview was being conducted around the launch of Berkley's personal website, Ask-Elizabeth.com, where she answers emails from teenage girls about body-image issues, dealing with stress, and family problems. (*Ask Elizabeth* was also the title of her 2011 self-help tome.) Berkley's bio on the website refers to her as an "accomplished actress" and cites her appearances on *CSI: Miami* and in films such as *The First Wives Club* (1996) and *Any Given Sunday* (1999). It does not mention *Showgirls*.

Berkley did indeed develop into an accomplished actress: she was excellent in her multi-episode arc on the Showtime drama *The L Word*, cast as a former college classmate (and obtuse object of desire) of the series protagonist Bette Porter, played, in a coincidence that had something of divine providence about it, by Jennifer Beals. (Both of Joe Eszterhas's dancing queens, together at last!) In 2008, Berkley started a gig as the host of a reality show on Bravo called *Step It Up and Dance*, wherein 12 aspiring dancers (both male and female) competed for a $100,000 prize. Berkley's comically poised, ultra-fierce demeanor hinted that she had embraced the disreputability of her *Showgirls* role, and there was something perversely satisfying in seeing Nomi Malone recast in the role of audition-room taskmaster a decade after her confrontation with Tony Moss. But while Berkley's stint on *Step It Up and Dance* might well have been therapeutic, it also had the ring of capitulation, or at best a Pyrrhic victory, clowning around in the ashes of a career that had very nearly self-immolated right out of the gate.

Nomi's rebirth/revenge is less ambiguous. As she hovers anxiously by Molly's bedside, her pal writhing in medication-induced unconsciousness, Nomi looks wounded to her core, and then adopts the hard, thousand-yard stare usually associated with action heroes. Verhoeven then cuts to Nomi applying her gladiatorial armor: silver and gold nail polish and blood red lipstick. Looking herself over in the mirror and liking what she sees, she gives herself a one-word pep talk: "Showtime."

Now *this* is what a masquerade looks like. Nomi is getting her game face on, and it's as fierce as her leopard-print miniskirt. Quentin Tarantino copped elements from this warrior-woman scene in *Inglourious Basterds* (2009), when Mélanie Laurent's Shosanna gets dolled up in red for her fateful movie premiere; indeed, Q.T.'s entire post–*Jackie Brown* (1997) output, with its obsessive focus on ice-cold revenge — call them "Gazpacho Westerns" — is deeply indebted to the final act of *Showgirls*. Verhoeven and Eszterhas were very much ahead of the pop-cultural curve here, as Nomi's encounter with Andrew Carver — sashaying into his hotel suite, disrobing, and then quite literally kicking the shit out of him — anticipates nearly identical scenes in both the Swedish and American movie versions of *The Girl with the Dragon Tattoo* (2009 and 2011).

This climax, it should be said, is an extremely satisfying scene, right down to the reappearance of Nomi's trusty switchblade, which she holds to the nasty rock star's throat before unleashing a wicked series of karate kicks that leave him prostrate on the floor. Nomi's assault is choreographed like a dance, as if she's finally mobilized her body and all its nervous, irrepressible energy in the service of a truly righteous act, an extended and far more vicious version of her little trick at the Crave Club where she kneed James in the groin for his impertinence.

It's hard to imagine that Tarantino wasn't paying Verhoeven a tribute in the final moments of *Death Proof* (2007), when Kurt Russell's serial-murdering misogynist gets gleefully battered to death by a trio of joy-riding riot grrrls. Tarantino routinely gets praised for his film's connections with the history of exploitation cinema, with critics clamoring to place *Kill Bill* (2003, 2004) in conversation with the collected works of Bo Anne Vinebius or to note *Death Proof*'s debt to *Vanishing Point* (1971) or *Faster, Pussycat! Kill! Kill!* (1965). Despite being released only a year after *Pulp Fiction* (1994), *Showgirls* was dismissed as if it had been written and directed in a vacuum. There was no thought spared for the possibility that Verhoeven and Eszterhas were similarly integrating grindhouse or rape-revenge-cinema tropes into their topless MGM musical.

That said, there does seem to be a little more at stake in these sequences, and Eszterhas went out of his way to make sure that everybody knew it. In an open letter to *Variety* published after *Showgirls*' dismal opening, Eszterhas wrote that "[*Showgirls*] shows that the dancers in Vegas are often victimized, humiliated, used, verbally and physically raped by the men who are at the power centers of that world . . . the advertising people have devised a tag line 'Leave Your Inhibitions at the Door' to sell a movie which is about a young woman who leaves her ambitions at the door to save her soul . . . I implore you not to let either misguided, fast-buck advertising . . . nor politically correct axe-grinding influence your feelings about *Showgirls* . . . I implore you to form your own conclusions."[60]

It's hard for a viewer to form his or her own conclusions, however, when a screenwriter is pleading in his or her ear. "[Eszterhas] should have known that . . . he was one of the most hated people in Hollywood," writes Rob Van Scheers. "The day of reckoning was always imminent."[61] Nomi Malone and Catherine Tramell are fictional characters; they can get revenge and get away with murder, respectively. Paul Verhoeven and Joe Eszterhas are filmmakers, and their power to contrive satisfying conclusions for their creations does not extend to their own real-life fortunes. The ice picks had been waiting under the bed since *Basic Instinct*, and after *Showgirls*, it was basically a contest to see who could plunge them in the deepest.

"He wants to sleep" is Nomi's winking, distaff-Schwarzenegger one-liner after dispatching Carver, followed immediately in the next scene by a nurse saying, "She's still out" with regard to Molly. Not only is Nomi the last woman standing, she's now portrayed as being wide-awake and wired, while the other characters are dazed and confused. Nomi leans over her sedated, puffy-eyed friend to tell her, "I kicked the fucking shit out of him," and is rewarded with a breathy, whispered "I love you," which immediately absolves Nomi of her sins. Molly exits the film much as she entered it: as a supportive friend who sees the best in a damaged young woman. That Nomi is indirectly responsible for her ordeal is an issue not long lingered on by either the characters or the filmmakers, who press on with their heroine's one-stop-shop forgiveness tour. Cristal, as it turns out, is convalescing just down the hall, and the score shifts into some drippy strings as Nomi enters to make peace and is confronted with the spectacle of the once-imposing Goddess in traction, yet still magisterial in her black cowboy hat.

Nomi is all apologies, but Cristal isn't buying it — or at least, not without a little haggling first. "Yeah, I know just how sorry you are," she smirks. "How do you think I got my first lead?" Nomi seems comforted rather than chastened by this revelation, and by Cristal's follow-up bit of bumper-sticker wisdom: "There's always someone younger and hungrier coming down the stairs after you." Nomi now knows that her rival's self-serving behavior wasn't a sign of a sick soul, but rather a symptom of showbiz; like Molly, Cristal generously doles out absolution from her hospital bed. She also invites Nomi to lean in for a "big kiss," which Verhoeven shoots romantically, even lingering on Gershon's credibly dewy-eyed face in its aftermath. Cristal hands Nomi her cowboy hat as a keepsake, completing the film-long transference between them: when Nomi leaves off with a lightly drawled "Goodbye, darlin'," it's not a competitive gesture, but rather imitation as the sincerest form of flattery.

Nomi and Cristal's mirror-mirror maneuvers are at an end, and so is the movie: the last scene repeats the blocking of the first, with Nomi hoisting her thumb on the highway at passing traffic. The blue pick-up truck that stops to get her is immediately familiar from the honky-tonk tunes blasting out the window, but it takes Jeff a moment to recognize Nomi in her cowboy hat and sunglasses. "So, did you gamble?" he asks her, and gets a big smile in return. "What did you win?" Nomi changes the radio to a rock station and lets Siouxsee predict her response for her, via the lyric of the Banshees' raucous "New Skin": "Fuck you, I win this prize." She then fixes Jeff with her newly confident gaze and answers for herself. "Me." Nomi is "no me" no more: she's won her name and her emancipation, and, with the help of her switchblade, she's going to get her possessions back too. "I want my fucking suitcase," she snarls, suggesting once again that Jeff is in for a long ride. As the camera drifts over a giant billboard proclaiming "Nomi Malone is Goddess," we can spy a sign that says that it's 280 miles to Los Angeles.

12

"They Don't Want to Fuck a Penny"

"I went into it thinking it would be a really erotic, serious, shocking exposé. People would be sitting on the edge of their seats. Maybe it's Verhoeven? Have you seen *Basic Instinct* lately? Even that seems campy now — I watched it last year, it wasn't the same movie I saw in the '90s. I think it's something with European filmmakers. I think — and this is my theory . . . there's something that European filmmakers have, a punched-up, extreme vibe. Everything's extreme."

— Rena Riffel,
in an interview with *Mondo Celluloid*,
March 2009

When we last see Penny, about two-thirds of the way through *Showgirls*, she's frowning at James after her desultory performance in his Crave Club showcase. She wants his approval that she did a good job, but as usual, he only has eyes for Nomi, who has either come to support or gloat about her promotion to the big leagues. Penny, as her name implies, is a cheap substitute, the sort of girl you can just pick up off the street. For James, she would seem to be a cursed piece of currency. Not only does she fail in her featured role as his blonde-bobbed muse, she gets herself knocked up to boot. "Shit happens," sighs James while informing Nomi of this latest development — hardly the words of a proud papa-to-be. In order to do right by his unlucky Penny, James is about to trade in his keys to the Crave Club (a name that connotes desire and inclusion) for a quotidian existence managing her father's grocery store. It's an ignominious ending for a character who had previously represented the allure of art for its own sweet sake.

As is so often the case in *Showgirls*, it's possible to see James's predicament in another way. Bedding Penny instead of waiting for Nomi may have been a matter of expedience (or sheer horniness), and yet it also allows James to exit the narrative before things get really bad for him. His attachment to Nomi has gotten him kicked in the balls and fired from a couple of menial jobs, but it's nothing compared to what Molly goes through by sticking with her friend to the bitter end. James probably suspects that he isn't going to make it in Las Vegas anyway, and so Penny could just as easily be his savior as his albatross, a shortcut to the American dream of home, business, and family. James's muted disappointment at being handed all of this prosperity on a silver platter is funny, and yet the comedy isn't really at his expense. Rather, his resignation to the fact that a better, more boring life awaits outside Las Vegas seems a bit like wisdom. Never having had the chance to get ahead, James is quitting while he's only slightly behind, cashing in his chips before he loses everything he has.

It will take Nomi several more scenes and a great deal of personal upheaval to reach some similar conclusions, but then the ending of *Showgirls* is provisional. No sooner has she "won" in Vegas then she seems willing to risk it all over again in Los Angeles. Whether or not Eszterhas and Verhoeven intend this ending to be strictly ironic is, once again, a question of how you look at it. Even if all roads do eventually lead back to show business, there is at least a possibility that Nomi will have learned enough from her Vegas adventure to avoid simply repeating her Pollyanna act in a new area code. And wouldn't it be fun to watch her kiss, connive, and kickbox her way through a whole new set of rivals? The billboard reading "Nomi Malone is Goddess" in the final shot of *Showgirls* is akin to the text that flashes across the screen at the end of every James Bond movie, reassuring us that 007 "will return."

While the idea of sequelized narratives is older than James Bond, Ian Fleming's superspy is the perfect avatar of the sequel mentality, which is to keep giving the audience what it wants at regular intervals, until the cost of producing new installments outweighs the rate of return on investment. In *Spaceballs* (1987), the wizened Yoda stand-in played by Mel Brooks closes a group pep talk by saying, "God willing we'll all meet again in *Spaceballs II: The Search for More Money*," a throwaway gag that skewered the title of *Star Trek III: The Search for Spock* (1984) in the middle of an extended *Star Wars* parody. From *Star Wars* to *Saw*, hit movies are liable to spawn sequels, and not only in the case of multiplex fare. But who would sequelize a Razzie-award-winning movie? A movie that wins a Razzie is perceived (not always fairly) to have been either very bad, very commercially unsuccessful, or both, and in all three instances, the wisdom of mounting a sequel would be questionable at best.

Showgirls 2: Penny's from Heaven is a sequel with nothing to lose, however. The film, which was released in 2012, is a calculated gamble by the intrepid Rena Riffel, who 15 years earlier had emerged from *Showgirls* unscathed, although not for lack of trying. Like Elizabeth Berkley, she had been groomed as an actress and a dancer from a young age, and just as Berkley read for the role of Kelly Kapowski on *Saved by the Bell* only to lose out, Riffel had Nomi Malone–ish designs on the part of Cristal Connors. Verhoeven decided that, at 26, Riffel was too young to play Cristal, but kept her around as Penny. Riffel is a nicely vivid presence in *Showgirls*: Penny's desperate need to impress everyone around her registers despite a lack of dialogue. Perhaps she was channeling her own experiences on the movie's set: Riffel pushed Verhoeven to include a song she'd recorded, entitled "Deep Kiss," on the movie's soundtrack; it made the cut during the lap-dance-threesome sequence.

One year later, Riffel appeared in a bit part in Andrew Bergman's *Striptease*, which took the Worst Picture Razzie trophy from *Showgirls* like a disgraced beauty pageant winner being handed a tarnished tiara. Bergman, a bright comic mind and student of film history who actually wrote a book on Depression-era Hollywood cinema — including the films of Busby Berkeley — before co-writing *Blazing Saddles* (1974) and *Fletch* (1985) and directing *The Freshman* (1990), had fallen into the same trap as Verhoeven in trying to make a movie that blended satirical comedy with sexually explicit material, although he did more to tip his hand. The problem with *Striptease* wasn't that people thought it was unintentionally funny: it was that they didn't think it was funny enough, Burt Reynolds's skilled performance as a scummy senator notwithstanding.

Just as *Showgirls'* heavy-bottomed budget was used against it as a kind of critical jujitsu, *Striptease* was sunk mostly by talk of money, chiefly the record $12.5 million paid to star Demi Moore, which was either in tribute to the box-office clout she'd earned after hits like *Ghost* (1990), *A Few Good Men* (1992), and *Indecent Proposal* (1993), or the Hollywood payday equivalent of the $500 slipped to Nomi Malone in exchange for that private dance.

Moore was a much bigger star than Elizabeth Berkley, but *Striptease* damaged her career in much the same way: appropriately enough for an actress who had just played Hester Prynne, *Striptease*'s terrible reviews and worse grosses branded her with a kind of scarlet letter. Just as Elizabeth Berkley's post-*Showgirls* career consisted of trying to completely disavow and then take revenge on the movie that had put her on the canvas, Moore made a series of reactionary moves, desexualizing herself entirely in Ridley Scott's *G.I. Jane* (1997), flexing a different set of acting muscles in the indie drama *Passion of Mind* (2000), and finally sending up her whole sexpot public image as the villain in *Charlie's Angels: Full Throttle* (2003), a winking bit of movie-star masquerade in a movie that made no bones about its camp orientation.

Rena Riffel, meanwhile, took a more secluded path, one that detoured down *Mulholland Drive* (2001). The title for David Lynch's comeback film could have just as easily been *Showgirls*, with unknowns Naomi Watts and Laura Elena Harring cast as aspiring actresses trying to make it in a strangely haunted version of Hollywood. The movie that Watts's Betty Elms auditions for has a strange sort of Busby Berkeley–ish sheen, and, like Nomi Malone, she'll do anything to get the part, including flirting with an older actor (Chad Everett) on the studio lot and making eyes at the director (Justin Theroux). At first, Betty's enthusiasm seems like a byproduct of youthful naïveté, but she isn't a Pollyanna: she's a Polly Ann Costello, right down to the small-town backstory. Actually, she's worse. All Nomi did was push somebody down the stairs. Betty — whose real name is Diane Selwyn — takes out a hit on her rival, who also happens to be her lover.

With its coterie of creepy casting agents and burlesque-club-of-the-damned imagery, *Mulholland Drive* could be *Showgirls'* malevolent and melancholy surrealist twin, if not its flipped mirror image. In both cases, the stars' performances are self-allegorizing: Watts was even more of an unknown at the time than Elizabeth Berkley, and her almost instantaneous jump to the A-list thereafter is the inverse of Berkley's precipitous fall. And in both movies, Rena Riffel is lurking in the background — in *Mulholland* as a heroin-addicted hooker who might also be an alternate embodiment of Betty/Diane. The main characters in *Mulholland Drive* are all obsessed with either finding or being "the Girl," but Riffel is just another pretty face.

That changes in *Showgirls 2*, where Riffel simultaneously occupies center stage and the director's chair. She didn't get there by accident: Riffel had been one of the public faces of *Showgirls'* camp reclamation in the early 2000s, appearing as a special guest at repertory screenings, including the hybrid movie/live-show events masterminded by the legendary San Francisco drag queen Peaches Christ, and giving interviews in which she argued that the movie had been misunderstood. Where Elizabeth Berkley fled, Rena Riffel lingered, and eventually, she decided to put down stakes in the wreckage and make a home (movie) for herself out of what was still standing.

Funded via Kickstarter and reportedly blessed by Verhoeven himself (even if he declined an invitation to participate), *Showgirls 2* is either an ambitious multi-hyphenate's idiosyncratic showcase, a jaw-dropping vanity project, or a little bit of both. Now gifted with the suggestive surname of "Slot" (even Joe Eszterhas might blush at that one), Penny finally emerges from Nomi's shadow, even as she follows in her stiletto-heeled footsteps. The underlying arc of *Showgirls 2* is the same as its predecessor, following a stars-in-her-eyes protagonist on a bumpy climb to the top of the showbiz ladder. The difference is that Riffel is doubling down on the ridiculousness. Not only does *Showgirls 2* kid the over-the-top aspects of *Showgirls*, with certain scenes from the original replayed as parody, but it also uses its predecessor's newly minted status as a camp landmark to indulge in all sorts of garish, non-sequitur silliness, from a trailer-park massacre initiated by a Marilyn Monroe impersonator to a scene in which a birthday cake is bludgeoned to bits by a demented prima ballerina.

The result is a film that's actually just around the corner from *Mulholland Drive*. While Riffel's references to *Showgirls* are relentless and detailed — she works in most of the original's most famous lines, and finds cameo roles for Glenn Plummer and Dewey Weber — the movie is too freewheelingly surreal to be pigeonholed simply as a send-up. Its cast is a veritable Lynch mob of freaks and oddities, including Shelley Michelle's Katya, who is ostensibly the Cristal Connors figure in the story but eventually splits the difference between Joan Crawford in *What Ever Happened to Baby Jane?* and Diane Ladd in Lynch's own *Wild at Heart* (1990). If the second half of *Mulholland Drive* is understandable as a subconscious "remake" of the first, replaying the idealized "dream" of Betty/Diane's Hollywood adventure as a guilt-ridden nightmare, *Showgirls 2* is like the fever dream of somebody who's overdosed on too many viewings of *Showgirls*. Call it "Nomi Malone Caffeine Pill Freakout."

Showgirls 2's aesthetics are pure YouTube, and it wears its cheap, tawdry production values (the budget was around $30,000) like a badge of honor, as if it was the Cheetah Club and *Showgirls* itself was the Stardust. And yet even that dichotomy is complicated since, just as the Cheetah's dancers desire to sell their bodies to a higher bidder, *Showgirls 2* desperately wants to get on the midnight-movie marquee alongside its predecessor. The whole movie is understandable as a two-and-a-half-hour elaboration of the shots in *Showgirls* where a mesmerized Nomi mimics Cristal's hand movements. Riffel has leveled her gaze directly at an absurd, excessive showbiz spectacle and decided that there's nothing she wants more than to climb onstage and start thrusting away alongside the Goddess, and maybe even to take her place.

"It was hard to tell if Riffel was trying to pay homage to the original, or to outright send it up," wrote the anonymous reviewer for the internet magazine *Crave Online*, and he's absolutely correct.[62] Whatever Riffel's reasons were for making the movie, the fact is that *Showgirls 2* is rife with contradictions. It's also one of the only sequels that lives up to Pauline Kael's ecstatic appraisal of *The Godfather Part II* (1974), which she claimed "enlarge[ed] the scope and deepen[ed] the meaning of the first film."[63] This is not to say that *Showgirls 2* is as good as *The Godfather: Part II*, or that it enlarges the scope or deepens the meaning of *Showgirls* in the same way that Francis Ford Coppola's sequel built off its Oscar-winning first installment. But its very existence as a popular midnight-movie attraction (it played theatrically in Los Angeles and made the genre-movie festival rounds across America) speaks to the increased visibility (and commercial viability) of *Showgirls* in the years after its release. Similarly, Riffel's contention in interviews that *Showgirls* was knowingly campy all along — which plays out in

Showgirls 2's defiantly garish vibe, with the director-star's performance a model example of sassy, gold-digging masquerade — vindicates certain of the film's admirers, reassuring them that it's finally okay to stop worrying and love the bomb. It might even be better to worship it, like those crazy cultists in *Beneath the Planet of the Apes* (1970).

Cultists will worship anything: hell, the revelers in The Who's 1969 rock opera *Tommy* based a religion around a pinball machine. In Pete Townshend's allegorical, phantasmagorical pop masterpiece, the only way for the deaf, dumb, and blind protagonist to gain emancipation from his demons is to smash his reflection in the mirror (actually, he gets his mom to do it for him). Nomi Malone performs a similar sort of image maintenance in *Showgirls* when she abandons her poster gal incarnation as the "Goddess" and walks away from Las Vegas on her own terms: her theme song could be Tommy's snarling "I'm Free." But while Penny gets farther and Riffel goes further than Nomi or Verhoeven ever did, her movie is ultimately trapped: it wants to be *Showgirls* and it wants to beat on *Showgirls*, and both goals are equally impossible. It can't ever smash the mirror, since it's nothing more than a refracted image to begin with. So its only recourse is to leer at is own reflection like a girl playing dress-up in her mother's clothes, lipstick smeared all over her face.

Riffel's film has been routinely described in feature articles and reviews as "campy," and yet it is not, not really. "If pure camp requires unawareness, then *Showgirls 2*'s script alone ensured it wouldn't hit the gold standard," writes Rich

Juzwiak. "It's more reminiscent of John Waters or Troma in its self-consciousness."[64] If, as so many critics thought at the time, *Showgirls* was true camp — a bad movie that didn't know it was a bad movie — then *Showgirls 2* is akin to one of those Hell's Kitchen kitsch-fests where the jeering members of the audience suddenly get to climb into the screen like Buster Keaton's *Sherlock Jr.* And if *Showgirls* wasn't true camp — if it was either self-consciously overwrought or deliberately stylized by its auteur — then *Showgirls 2* seems equally redundant: a send-up of a send-up, a parody of a parody.

Riffel isn't responsible for what Verhoeven's film is or is not, but the fact that *Showgirls 2* can't seem to decide for itself whether it's putting *Showgirls* down or putting it on a pedestal is how it actually ends up deepening the original's meaning. Riffel oscillates wildly between tribute and travesty with the same gawky clumsiness as Nomi Malone at the Crave Club. She can't tell the difference between loving and hating *Showgirls* any more than Nomi could figure out the distinction between dancing and fucking. Even if she has her heart and soul in both ventures (as Nomi did), that sense of slippage is enough to drive anybody crazy. It leaves our filmmaker (or our filmgoer) at the mercy of the two angels perched on her shoulder, one loudly proclaiming, "Piece of Shit" with a French accent, while the other slyly whispers, "Masterpiece."

13

"It Doesn't Suck"

As Molly so quickly intuited upon meeting Nomi back in the Riviera's parking lot, the girl doesn't really have much experience with people being nice to her. And most of the people she meets in Las Vegas aren't nice to her either. Jeff steals her suitcase; Al forces her to perform a lap dance against her will; James tells her that she can't dance and that she's a pain in his ass; Tony Moss makes her rub ice cubes all over her chest; Zack has sex with her and then threatens her with indentured servitude at the Stardust; Andrew Carver makes an ugly pass at her and then rapes her best friend; Cristal humiliates her at every turn and even pimps her out by proxy. At the same time, though, Nomi gets plenty of compliments over the course of the film: about her dancing, about her nails, about her breasts (on three separate occasions), and about how good she looks in her new Ver-sayce dress. Nomi's response to the latter is simply to say: "It doesn't suck."

For Nomi, who has been through so much in her previous life as Polly Ann Costello, this is as close as it gets to glass-half-full thinking. She uses exactly the same words to describe Cristal when she brushes by her in the hallway during the *Goddess* press conference, and also to comment on the cheeseburger that James buys her during their sunny afternoon idyll. In a way, "It doesn't suck" is her mantra even more than "I'm a dancer" or "Shit happens." Those are, respectively, delusions of grandeur and a t-shirt mantra, unfettered naïveté and faux-worldliness. But "It doesn't suck" fits Nomi as snugly as that Versace dress: it looks good on her, and yet it doesn't require her to put on airs. When she says it, she sounds like she means it.

Fittingly for a character who wears several faces over the course of *Showgirls* — naïf, newbie, vamp, vixen, avenging angel — and is called by nearly as many names (Heather, Pollyanna, Polly Ann, Goddess), Nomi sometimes seems to lose herself in her environment, to forget who she's supposed to be at a given moment or fail to understand what's expected of her. She is at once the strongest and the weakest character in *Showgirls*, the one who catalyzes fear and desire in everyone she meets and yet who remains vulnerable to their machinations and manipulations, as well as her own deep-seated insecurities — starting with her suspicion that no matter how much people seem to want a piece of her, she is alone in the world.

The *picaros*, or feminine *picaras*, of literary history are often, but not always, orphans whose essential loneliness compels them to try to either locate a surrogate family or break into the larger society around them. *Picaras* are strivers, resilient, solitary figures who must survive in a confusing social landscape with hypocritical, deceptive, and uncertain surfaces. Their endearing qualities become foregrounded against these comically nightmarish backdrops, and yet they are themselves frequently inconstant: easily duped, swayed, or led astray. The *picara* is a blank slate who will come to discover virtues, but no matter what she learns of life (and no matter how hard the lesson), she will retain a certain static innocence. She is a contradictory character, who must be endearing enough that we root for her to overcome the obstacles in her path, but also so driven and ambitious that she perseveres instead of choosing a safer route or abandoning the journey altogether.

Paul Verhoeven has an affinity for picaresque protagonists, and it's no wonder: he himself is a sort of picaresque figure, forever pressing his luck and achieving success before wearing out his welcome and being forcibly ejected from the party. And yet it would be hard to say that Verhoeven has been especially ill-treated in his career, since his problems with censors, critics, audiences, and collaborators on both sides of the Atlantic are directly connected to the confrontational aspects of his cinema. Time and again, he plumbs the depths of bad taste and is called out for it; like any good *picaro*, Verhoeven's inability to learn his lesson is at once admirable and self-defeating. While his slick, acidic films are surely not naïve, his unwavering faith in his own abilities and in his mandate to give audiences exactly what they want (even if they won't admit it) bespeak a kind of integrity.

Unlike Joe Eszterhas, who second-guessed his own work on *Basic Instinct* and then tried to guilt the populace into taking *Showgirls* as seriously as he insisted it deserved to be, Verhoeven makes movies fearlessly, and the extreme reactions he provokes — worship and excoriation, sometimes in very close proximity — are in proportion to the extreme pitch of his artistry.

"The theme of redemption is part of American mythology," writes Verhoeven in the conclusion to his essay in *Showgirls: Portrait of a Film*. "American movies are filled with these fairy tales in which everything comes out right and everybody goes to the seashore. It is an illusion that is supported by the whole culture, and is probably part of the larger unwillingness to look at unpleasant realities."[65] At times, Verhoeven's American films analyze and satirize this willful blindness — think of Quaid's climactic embrace of the synapse-frying Martian fantasy over his workaday life in *Total Recall*, or Nick mouthing nonsense about happily ever after in *Basic Instinct* — and yet the director proved no less susceptible to the lure of such magical thinking. On the eve of his greatest failure, the émigré perfectionist believed that he had found a new home in Hollywood.

"I have a much different rhythm when I work here than when I worked in Holland," Verhoeven continues in *Portrait of a Film*. "In my country things are much grayer. In the United States there is more contrast, more social and political tension. More drama. More fun! I suppose that if my films reflect that tension, and even if they provoke strong responses, I fulfill some function an artist. Perhaps, now, as an American artist."[66] *Showgirls'* account of a dancer who is mistaken at every turn for a whore, and who nearly loses her soul before finding it once and for all — and who kicks the shit out of her tormentors for good measure — may finally be understandable as Verhoeven's allegorical account of his own picaresque adventures in his adopted homeland.

The difference is that Nomi leaves town on her own terms, while Verhoeven the *picaro* was basically cast out, with nobody to beat up but himself. Notwithstanding the relative success of *Starship Troopers*, which had been initiated before *Showgirls* irreparably damaged his brand, his follow-up *Hollow Man* (2000) paints a pretty persuasive self-portrait of the director coping with his impending self-exile: its Invisible-Man-gone-mad gimmick is the pretense for a character study of a brilliant creep who feels himself disappearing into thin air. Verhoeven's redemption would come not on American soil, but back in Holland, where the prodigal son was received with approbation.

Not that Verhoeven finally capitulated to the windmill-and-dike tradition: with *Black Book*, he managed to combine the scathing sociological critique of his earlier Dutch features with the double-barreled blockbuster intensity of his American movies, and even threw a blonde showgirl in there for good measure. Carice van Houten's resourceful Rachel Stein only wants to be a singer, but ends up working as a spy for anti-Nazi Dutch partisans, a Jewish Mata Hari manqué who survives her double life and ends up as a sort of homecoming queen.

With its severely unflattering portrayal of Dutch resistance fighters as anti-Semitic and unsettling images of Nazi collaborators being shorn and tortured by their countrymen after the end of World War II, *Black Book* is no less excoriating a social vision than *Spetters*. Unlike its predecessor, however, it was not picketed or protested: rather, it was chosen as Holland's submission for the Academy Award for Best Foreign Language Film in 2006, and grossed more money than any other homegrown film in the country's history. In 2008, it was voted the best Dutch movie ever made in a poll organized by the Netherlands Film Festival. Verhoeven seemed to have been granted the grace that is bestowed by age.

The name of the game, then, is endurance: to wait things out until you're on the right side of history. "There are a number of reasons to consider bad movies," writes J. Hoberman. "The most obvious is that tastes change; that many, if not most of the films we admire were once dismissed as inconsequential trash; and that trash itself is not without its socio-aesthetic charms."[67] He's not describing *Showgirls* here, but his words fit. The increasing critical vogue for ironic pop-cultural appreciation and "vulgar auteurism" — a mode of critical practice that applies the previously rarified Truffautian criteria for great, personal cinema to the rascally likes of Tony Scott, John Carpenter, and those (s)avant-garde juvenalian delinquents Neveldine/Taylor of *Crank* (2006) fame — has created a context where a movie previously judged an abject failure might be reclaimed as a roaring success, one worthy of that old MGM lion after all.

The liberating possibilities of this approach are obvious, but the danger is that the critic begins looking back through rose-colored glasses, and objects in the rearview mirror appear larger and more substantial than they really are. But *Showgirls* truly was too big in every way to simply vanish over the horizon. Imagine trying to drive far enough away from a mushroom cloud that it fades from view. The film's toxic fallout has mostly receded, and while the air around the detonation site is still murky, life has found a way. Those Strangeloveian bomb-worshippers have turned the crater into Ground Zero for an entire thriving subculture, a full-dress pagan dance party in honor of their chosen Goddess. Linda Williams's prophecy that "*Showgirls* will re-emerge . . . like Nomi and Cristal from their papier-mâché volcano, in triumphant glory to gain the praise that it deserves" has come true.

A notable American statesman immortalized onscreen by Steven Spielberg claimed, "At 40, you get the face that you deserve." Now that *Showgirls* is all of 19 years old (not even old enough to dance with, according to Steely Dan) does this mean that it's getting the praise that it deserves? One can almost hear that other famed American icon, Clint Eastwood, growling in response: "Deserve's got nothing to do with it." For many, *Showgirls*' sins—and all of the seven deadly ones are in there, somewhere — will be forever unforgiven.

But a case can be made — and hopefully has been here — that Verhoeven and co. were brought in on ludicrously trumped-up charges in the first place. Double jeopardy laws are there to protect people from being charged twice for the same crime, and yet it seems that *Showgirls* took the rap for *Basic Instinct*, with reviewers banding together to make a citizen's arrest. The eyewitness accounts that got the movie convicted now appear deeply flawed. It's as if critics were looking at the film's funhouse distortions of American film history with eyes wide shut — or else blind to the admittedly rare spectacle of a movie where the mirror truly has two faces.

Showgirls is guilty of many things, your honor, but at the end of the day, doesn't premeditation count for something? If the defendant has a history of making movies with malice aforethought, should we not consider his permanent record? Making one of the worst movies of all time may be the only thing that Paul Verhoeven is innocent of, but facts are facts, and *Showgirls* has just enough of them on its side to hang even the most determined jury.

Back in that Parisian apartment, the argument about the movie circles around and around in an infernal loop. The cries of "Masterpiece" and "Piece of Shit" go back and forth until they blend together; listen carefully and it might even sound like they're saying "Masterpiece of Shit," a portmanteau that just might have to do for a final verdict. For now, there's an awful lot of racket here. But turn down the volume a bit and we can hear Paul — an auteurist, but also a peacemaker — speaking words of wisdom.

> *I'd take the middle road: it's not the piece of junk critics said it was when it came out. It's still Verhoeven, but not one of his better ones.*

Or, to quote another Paul: "Pretty good, huh?"

Well, it doesn't suck.

*Notes

1 I.Q. Hunter, "Beaver Las Vegas: A Fan Boy's Defense of *Showgirls*," *The Cult Film Reader*, ed. Ernest Mathijs and Xavier Mendik (New York: Open University Press, 2007), 45.

2 *Sight & Sound* Greatest Films poll, results from David Panos, http://explore.bfi.org.uk/sightandsoundpolls/2012/voter/929.

3 Susan Sontag, "Notes on 'Camp,'" *Against Interpretation and Other Essays* (New York: Farrar, Straus, and Giroux, 1966), accessed online at http://www9.georgetown.edu/faculty/irvinem/theory/sontag-notesoncamp-1964.html.

4 Trip Gabriel, "*Showgirls* Crawls Back as High Camp at Midnight," *The New York Times*, March 31, 1996.

5 Anthony Lane, "Starkness Visible," *The New Yorker*, October 9, 1995, 95.

6 Kate Torgovnick, "Razzie Nominations: The 5 Famous Folks Who've Accepted Their Awards in Person," *The Frisky*, January 24, 2011, http://www.thefrisky.com/2011-01-24/razzie-nominations-the-five-famous-folks-whove-accepted-their-awards-in/.

7 Gabriel, "*Showgirls* Crawls Back as High Camp at Midnight."

8 Joe Eszterhas, *The Devil's Guide to Hollywood* (New York: St Martin's, 2006), 352.

9 Charles Taylor, "Alive and Kicking," *Salon*, March 31, 2004, http://www.salon.com/2004/03/31/showgirls_2/.

10 Frédéric Bonnaud, "The Captive Lover: An Interview with Jacques Rivette," *Senses of Cinema* 16 (September 2001) http://sensesofcinema.com/2001/16/rivette-2/.

11 Paul Verhoeven, *Showgirls: Portrait of a Film* (New York: Newmarket Press, 1995), 15.

12 Jeffrey Sconce, "I Have Grown Weary of Your Tiresome Cinema," *Film Quarterly* 56, no. 3 (Spring 2003), 44.

13 Pauline Kael, "Fatal Attraction," *Hooked* (New York: Plume, 1989), 377.

14 Richard Corliss, "Valley of the Dulls," *Time*, October 16, 1995, 40.

15 Rob Van Scheers, *Paul Verhoeven* (London: Faber and Faber, 1997), 244.

16 Eszterhas, *The Devil's Guide to Hollywood*, 58–59.

17 Van Scheers, *Paul Verhoeven*, 248.

18 Jay Scott, review of *Basic Instinct*, *Great Scott! The Best of Jay Scott's Movie Reviews*, ed. Karen York (Toronto: McClelland & Stewart, 1994), 334.

19 Van Scheers, *Paul Verhoeven*, 24.

20 *Ibid*, 135.

21 Scott, review of *Basic Instinct*, 334–335.

22 Verhoeven, *Showgirls: Portrait of a Film*, 8.

23 *Ibid*.

24 Eszterhas, *The Devil's Guide to Hollywood*, 179.

25 Larissa MacFarquhar, "Start the Lava," *Premiere* (October 1995), 84.

26 Von Scheers, *Paul Verhoeven*, 264.

27 *Ibid*, 262.

28 McFarquhar, "Start the Lava," 84.

29 Verhoeven, *Showgirls: Portrait of a Film*, 12.

30 *Ibid*, 13.

31 Janet Maslin, "40 Million Worth of Voyeurism," *The New York Times*, September 22, 1995.

32 Chon Noriega, "A Whisper of Satire," *Film Quarterly* 56, no. 3 (Spring 2003), 37.

33 Van Scheers, *Paul Verhoeven*, 261.

34 Eric Schaefer, "*Showgirls* and the Limits of Sexploitation," *Film Quarterly* 56, no. 3 (Spring 2003), 42.

35 Verhoeven, *Showgirls: Portrait of a Film*, 9.

36 Van Scheers, *Paul Verhoeven*, 263.

37 Bernard Weinraub, "Big Film Gets NC-17, and Studio Backs It," *The New York Times*, July 21, 1995.

38 William Grimes, "In the Wings: A Movie With Few Clothes and No Regrets," *The New York Times*, February 12, 1995.

39 *Ibid*.

40 *Ibid*.

41 Bill Krohn, review of *Showgirls*, *Cashiers du Cinema* 498 (January 1996), 81.

42 Kevin Sandler, "The Naked Truth: *Showgirls* and the Fate of the NC-17 Rating," *Cinema Journal* 40, no 3. (Spring 2001), 80.

43 *Ibid*, 85.

44 *Ibid*, 83.

45 Lane, "Starkness Visible," 96.

46 Linda Williams, "*Showgirls* and Sex Acts," *Film Quarterly* 56, no. 3 (Spring 2003), 40.

47 Pamela Robertson, "What Trixie and God Know," *Guilty Pleasures: Feminist Camp from Mae West to Madonna* (Durham and London: Duke University Press, 1996), 62.

48 Williams, "*Showgirls* and Sex Acts," 41.

49 Rick Groen, review of *Showgirls*, *The Globe and Mail*, September 22, 1995.

50 Maslin, "$40 Million Worth of Voyeurism."

51 Owen Gleiberman, review of *Starship Troopers*, *Entertainment Weekly*, October 13, 1997.

52 Noriega, "A Whisper of Satire," 37.

53 Lester Haines, "*Showgirls* clinches worst movie sex scene award," *The Register*, September 30, 2005, http://www.theregister.co.uk/2005/09/30/worst_movie_romp/.

54 Verhoeven, *Showgirls: Portrait of a Film*, 65.

55 Vincent Canby, "*Spetters* Views Dutch Motorcycle Riders," *The New York Times*, February 8, 1981.

56 Ulrich Wicks, *Picaresque Narrative, Picaresque Fictions: A Theory and Research Guide* (London: Greenwood, 1989), 65.

57 Mary Ann Doane, "Film and the Masquerade: Theorizing the Female Spectator," *Issues in Feminist Film Criticism*, ed. Patricia Eren (Indianapolis: Indiana University Press, 1990), 44.

58 Ara Osterweil, "A Fan's Notes on Camp, Or How I Learned to Stop Worrying and Love *Showgirls*," *Film Quarterly* 56, no. 3 (Spring 2003), 9.

59 Verhoeven, *Showgirls: Portrait of a Film*, 12.

60 Van Scheers, *Paul Verhoeven*, 273.

61 *Ibid.*

62 William Bibbiani, review of *Showgirls 2: Penny's From Heaven*, *Crave Online*, November 11, 2011, http://www.craveonline.com/film/reviews/177901-review-showgirls-2-pennys-from-heaven.

63 Pauline Kael, "The Godfather, Part II: Fathers and Sons," *The New Yorker*, December 23, 1974.

64 Rich Juzwiak, "So Weird, It's Weird: *Showgirls 2* Doesn't Suck," *Gawker*, April 12, 2012, http://gawker.com/5901364/so-weird-its-weird-showgirls-2-doesnt-suck.

65 Verhoeven, *Showgirls: Portrait of a Film*, 12.

66 *Ibid.*

67 J. Hoberman, "Bad Movies," *American Movie Critics: An Anthology from the Silents Until Now*, ed. Phillip Lopate (New York: Penguin, 2006), 517.

Acknowledgments

I must begin by thanking Crissy Calhoun and Jennifer Knoch, my stalwart editors at ECW Press. The Pop Classics series is their baby and I did what I could to avoid being a problem child. The rest of the team at ECW did their best to get this book out of my brain, onto the page, and then onto the shelves — some enthusiastic jazz hands are due to David Caron, Erin Creasey, Jack David, Sarah Dunn, Troy Cunningham, David Gee, Avril McMeekin, and Michelle Melski, among others.

I wrote most of my book at the TIFF Film Reference Library, under the watchful eye of head honcho Eve Goldin. A shout-out also to her crack staff: Kristen MacDonald, Rachel Beattie, Sagan Yee, and Alannah Fotheringham, who always kept the "big box of *Showgirls* stuff" close at hand. Despite their heavy loads taking and teaching classes respectively, David Davidson and Katherine Quanz both did valuable volunteer legwork locating and scanning key documents.

Thank you to TIFF Bell Lightbox's director of programming Jesse Wente for arranging a special screening of *Showgirls* coinciding with the launch of this book. Extra-special thanks to TIFF Cinematheque stalwarts Brad Deane and Lina Rodriguez for their interest in the project, and for arranging my dinner with Mia Hansen-Løve, who kindly consented to let me reprint a section of her original screenplay (*merci beaucoup*, Mia).

I'm fortunate to have so many good friends and colleagues who were willing to talk about *Showgirls* with me over the last year and a half: thanks to Fernando Croce, Simon Ennis, Sarah Fobes, Jocelyn Geddie, Marc Glassman, Kieran Grant, Tina Hassannia, Eric Hynes, Danny Kasman, Robert Koehler, Michael Koresky, Ray Lahey, Phil Leers, Aliz Ma, Calum Marsh, Cameron Moneo, Alex Molennaar, Angelo Muredda, Liora Norwich, Mark Peranson, Mariapia Pietropalo, Jeff Reichert, David Schwartz, Jennifer Scott, Amanda Shubert, John Semley, Girish Shambu, Robyn Stanwyck, Mark Slutsky, Jose Teodoro, Norman Wilner, Cam Woykin and Claire Zaya.

Portions of this book originally appeared in an essay I wrote at the University of Toronto for Professor Corinn Columpar, and I am just one of many former students who is grateful to have been taught by her.

Jason Anderson is a beloved colleague, and he helped this book in several ways, including as an impromptu entertainment lawyer (*pro bono*, no less).

A few years ago, Esther Arbeid invited me to teach film appreciation classes at the Miles Nadal JCC, and the lecture I did on Paul Verhoeven was formative to the creation of this book. She's still the only person I consistently refer to as my boss.

Danelle Eliav is a constant source of wisdom and

encouragement. Kiva Reardon and Darrah Teitel are both terrific writers and treasured friends who gave me feedback when it mattered.

Kevin Courrier makes a cameo appearance in my fourth chapter, and there is nobody I like talking about movies with more.

Ever since he handed back one of my second-year film studies papers with the comment "this is well written" and a grade of C-plus, Bart Testa has been my toughest editor and critic. I hope he knows how much I appreciate it.

Andrew Tracy did far more than he had to whip this book into shape. Please direct any particularly effusive compliments about its structure and substance in his direction. (You may address all criticisms to me.)

Sandra, Vesa, and Michael Koivusalo have been treating me like family since long before it was official, and I'm always thankful for their support. If I start thanking Matthew Nayman and Suzie Lowe for everything they've done for me, I'll go over my word count.

My parents, David Nayman and Evelyne Michaels, have always been proud of me, even when I announced I was publishing a book on *Showgirls*. I love them for that and for a few other things too.

Like most of the things in my life, this book would be unthinkable without the input, indulgence, advice, attention and love I get every day from my wife, Tanya Koivusalo. She definitely doesn't suck.

Adam Nayman is a film critic in Toronto for *The Grid* and the *Globe and Mail* and a contributing editor to *Cinema Scope*. He has written on film for the *Village Voice*, *L.A. Weekly*, *Film Comment*, *Cineaste*, *Montage*, *POV*, *Reverse Shot*, *The Walrus*, *Saturday Night*, and *Little White Lies*. He teaches film studies at the University of Toronto and Ryerson University and is a programmer for the Toronto Jewish Film Society. He lives in Toronto, Ontario.

At ECW Press, we want you to enjoy this book in whatever format you like, whenever you like. Leave your print book at home and take the eBook to go! Purchase the print edition and receive the eBook free. Just send an email to ebook@ecwpress.com and include:

- the book title
- the name of the store where you purchased it
- your receipt number
- your preference of file type: PDF or ePub?

A real person will respond to your email with your eBook attached. And thanks for supporting an independently owned Canadian publisher with your purchase!